While this book is essentially biographical, I hope it also reflects my tremendous admiration and respect for the United States Marine Corps. I am here by the grace of God and the fighting skills of these courageous young men. I hope never again to be surrounded by powerful, well-armed, and well-trained enemy forces, but if that be my fate, let it be in the company of Marines.

In the Company of Marines
A Surgeon Remembers Vietnam

James O. Finnegan, MD

Copyright 2009
ISBN: 978–0-557–06639
Library of Congress Control Number: 2009907403

Contents

Foreword

On a September day in 1967 a young surgeon boarded a plane at Philadelphia International Airport and headed off to war. Like many young men of his generation, Dr. Jim Finnegan could hardly have been branded an ideologue. "I had no particular knowledge of why we were fighting, no understanding of the threat of communism, and certainly no concept of where in the world Vietnam was located or why it was so important." What was important was that his nation was at war; men even younger than he were fighting and dying on the far side of the world, and his surgical skills could help save some of them. Thus begins the very personal and often searing recollections of a combat surgeon's year in Vietnam.

And 1968 was quite a year. Although the first American combat troops had arrived in Vietnam in 1965, since then, the United States had become deeply mired in the conflict. By 1968, troop levels had reached 536,000 with only modest success to show in defeating mostly home-grown Viet Cong guerrillas and the well-trained, highly motivated, and Chinese- and Soviet-equipped North Vietnamese Army. As 1968 entered its second month, the communists launched the infamous Tet offensive. Cities and towns all across South Vietnam erupted in a crescendo of violence that stunned Americans who witnessed the graphic bloodletting on the evening news day after day. The brutal twenty-six-day battle for Hue, which killed at least ten thousand Vietnamese and nearly two hundred Americans, soon competed for attention with the siege of an isolated outpost near the Laotian border called Khe Sanh. Lt. Jim Finnegan had begun his Vietnam tour of duty at a medical company called "Delta Med." To the casual observer it was *M*A*S*H* without the attractive nurses. But Delta Med was also a rude awakening for a surgeon who had never seen such horribly wounded and mutilated men. No civilian experience could have prepared him for what he witnessed—burns, traumatic amputations, fatal head wounds, gunshot wounds to the torso, head, and neck— all inflicted by high-velocity automatic weapons, mines, rocket-propelled grenades, mortars, and artillery. Yet this was but an initiation for what was to come.

Four months later, Finnegan jumped off a Huey gunship that had just landed at the Khe Sanh combat base to become the new commanding officer of "Charlie Med," the base's main medical facility. It was a true "from the frying pan into the fire" experience. Beginning in mid-January and lasting through April

1968, an estimated twenty to forty thousand North Vietnamese troops besieged the combat base. Finnegan and his fellow medical personnel would not only endure the epic seventy-seven-day siege but end up treating more than twenty-five hundred casualties without the benefit of x-ray machines, monitoring equipment, and what would be considered essential for any community hospital back in the states. And this heroic medical care was delivered while braving thousands of incoming shells each day.

Over forty years have passed since the events and memories described in this book. Newer conflicts have come and gone, and even though the nation is at war both in Iraq and Afghanistan, for my generation, at least, the Vietnam experience is still very much a part of us. *In the Company of Marines: A Surgeon Remembers Vietnam* makes it all very real for everyone else.

Jan K. Herman
Washington, DC
January 30, 2009

Preface

I'm on the beach. There's a cool breeze on my face, the waves are lapping on the shore—such a peaceful sound. I'm dreaming of beautiful women, whiskey, and song. The sun is just above the horizon. Is it rising or setting? I can't tell. The scene is one of peace and I feel complete contentment. Suddenly, the sun is hotter; the noise around me louder. I am pulled out of my reverie and realize that this was all a dream. I'm not on a beach. There are no waves, no peace or contentment, definitely no beautiful women. I had fallen asleep. Where am I? Oh no. I'm laying on the grass outside of a cyclone fence surrounding the fighter jet parking revetments at the Da Nang airfield. Staring me in the face are the afterburners of an F-14 fighter plane that is about to take off on a mission over NorthVietnam.

This is my introduction to Vietnam.

Acknowledgements

The chapter in this book about Dr. Ed Feldman tells the story of a true medical hero. He has been nominated for the Medal of Honor and hopefully will receive it in his lifetime. But there were many others who cared for Marine casualties under the extremely adverse tactical circumstances (in "Marinespeak" that means that there existed a very high risk of getting your ass shot off). Two of them remain my good friends. Dr. Joe Cesare, the best orthopedic surgeon I know, has never asked for or received the recognition he so richly deserves for all of the casualty care he provided in Vietnam. Dr. Jim Thomas, now a professor and chairman of a department of surgery, served on the frontline with the "grunts" and operated on many of the wounded. Dr. Joe Wolfe, our "anesthesiologist," stood firm during the siege. I wish I could mention everyone who gave so much. You know who you are.

Jan Herman, the longtime editor of *Navy Medicine,* has been a friend, advisor, and reader of this manuscript. His heartfelt encouragement and guidance were invaluable.

My father, James A., is responsible for my love of education and my patriotism. God rest him.

Louis A. Pinola is my father-in-law, my friend, and a fellow Navy veteran. Without him and his wife, Gemma, there would be no Linda, and without Linda, there would be no book.

Dedications

Note the plural—this book has been "in me" for a long, long time. It took a lot of love, encouragement, friendship, and personal loss to get me to the point where I actually was able to sit down and begin to write. This book is dedicated to all those who got me there and I'm going to tell you something about each of them. I look upon "Dedications" as chapter one of this book.

If I chose to limit the dedication to one person, it would be my lovely and loving wife, Linda. She has been my main motivator, to say nothing of "at-home" editor, chief typist, scanner, and organizer. She watched me struggle through my early attempts to learn how to use the laptop computer she bought for me. Word processing may seem the simplest of all computer applications to many, but to me, a "discover and land" typist (the Columbus method), it was a daunting task. She never stopped encouraging me and took great personal satisfaction in watching my progress. If you are reading this in book form, it is because of her. I love you, Babe.

When I left for Vietnam, my children were too young to know or understand what I was doing. Today, they do know, and do understand. Hopefully, the fifteen grandchildren they produced will also understand someday. Maybe this book will help. I'd like you to at least read their names, listed here in birth order with their families:

Mark and Joanne Finnegan and their sons, Sean, Kevin, Danny, and Timmy;

Matt and Katie Finnegan and their kids, Brendan and Bridget;

Maureen and Mark Edelson plus Ryan, Genevieve, Mary Kate, Maggie, and Angela-Michael

Martin and Patty Finnegan plus Owen, Liam, Annie Kathleen, and Michael.

I love them all.

Missing from the list of family members is my son Michael, who died quite suddenly in December of 2002 at the young age of thirty-nine. Here's a little something I wrote about him one day when I was sitting at my desk thinking of him, something I do quite frequently.

What I Know About Michael

I know that he renovated a room or did a major repair in just about everybody's home.

I know the proudest moment of his life was the day he purchased his first home and immediately brought his ninety-year-old grandmother to live with him so he could take care of her.

I know he loved cars, all cars, but probably none as much as the Mercury Cougar he had as a teenager.

I know that he loved his family more than anything and would and did do anything any of them asked of him (usually accompanied by a liberal measure of complaint and criticism).

I know he loved golf and could hit a four wood over 250 yards, although not necessarily into the intended fairway.

I know that he was very proud of his graduations from Malvern Prep and Lehigh University, but not particularly fond of the book work it took to attain those goals.

I know that he loved me because he was always there for me, especially in difficult times.

And I know that wherever he may be physically, he is spiritually, intellectually and emotionally here with me now.

Michael Patrick Finnegan 8/16/63–12/10/02
Mike at the Presidential inauguration—January, 2002

And for that soon-to-be well-known artist, my daughter Caitlin Elizabeth, "Catie Patatie," whose portrait sketch of me as a young naval officer just out of Vietnam brought tears to my eyes and gave me the boost I needed to sit down and write this book. You go girl.

Portrait of the author
drawn by his daughter Caitlin.

Chapter One

Some Little-Known Facts About The Vietnam Conflict

There have been literally thousands of articles written about the plight of Vietnam veterans. Many of the stories emphasize such things as unemployment, drug usage, and psychological issues. Less well known but easily available to anyone interested in the topic are the many positive stories about the veterans of that unpopular war. For example:

- One out of every ten Americans who served in Vietnam was a casualty. Of the 2.7 million who served, 58,260 were killed and 304,000 wounded. The average age of the KIAs (killed in action) was 23.1 years, and 61 percent were younger than 21. Of those killed, 50,274 (86.3 percent) were enlisted, averaging 23.11 years old.

- Seventy-five thousand were severely disabled, with 23,214 of those 100 percentdisabled.

- There are still 1,875 Americans unaccounted for from the Vietnam War.

- Two hundred forty men were awarded the Medal of Honor during the Vietnam War.

- Ninety-seven percent of Vietnam veterans were honorably discharged; 91 percent say they are glad they served; 74 percent say they would serve again, even knowing the outcome.

- Vietnam veterans have a lower unemployment rate than the same nonveteran age groups. Vietnam veterans' personal income exceeds that of our nonveteran age group by more than 18 percent.

- Eighty percent of Vietnam veterans made successful transitions to civilian life. Vietnam veterans are less likely to be in prison—only one half of 1 percent have been jailed for crimes. There is no difference in drug usage between Vietnam veterans and non–Vietnam veterans of the same age group.

Chapter Two

Vietnam From the Beginning

I thought I could write the story of Charlie Med at Khe Sanh as an isolated tale. It just doesn't work that way for me. As important as Khe Sanh was, it somehow requires context if one is to appreciate the full impact of the siege. I don't mean the military events leading up to this much-publicized battle, but rather the personal circumstances that caused me to be there. I have the certain feeling that there are very few people on God's green earth who will give one tiny damn about my stories, but I am determined to commit them to paper in the hope that at the very least, it will help my friends and family to know what I did and why I did it.

I am certainly not, at this point in my life, looking for approval of what I did. No. Wait. Stop. That's not true and I've promised myself that this would be nothing but the truth.

I want very much for someone, anyone to hear me out and say "great job" or "you guys were awesome" or "thank you"— some evidence that what we did is accorded some importance and respect.

Medals are nice and I love receiving them, ceremonies are nice and I love attending them, but of far greater importance to me is that our story is told and preserved in an honorable fashion. I don't want the wounds, the deaths, the Marines, the Navy corpsmen, the Navy surgical team of doctors, and all of the heroic moments that make up the story of the Third Medical Battalion of the Third Marine Division in Vietnam *ever* to be forgotten.

Much has been written about the alleged bad judgment that resulted in a conflict that cost the lives of over fifty-eight thousand men. Serious questions have been raised about the tactics employed by some of our top generals in dealing with the Vietcong and NVA (North Vietnamese Army). While I am aware of those discussions and dismayed that we spent over ten years fighting what many felt was an unwinnable war, I must confess that in early 1967 when I made the decision to relinquish my deferment and volunteer for duty in Vietnam, I did not have a political or military thought in my head. I simply did not want to miss the war. That statement obviously requires an explanation, lest you think that I was just a young man with a quest for adventure and an unquenched thirst for action. Let me tell you about my father.

When the Japanese bombed Pearl Harbor on December 7, 1941, my father was already twenty-seven years old and had two kids—my sister and me. He worked at a steel mill in Pittsburgh, Pennsylvania, which was in the process of being converted from the production of civilian steel products to a full-scale military manufacturer. He was already the foreman in charge of an area that was being converted to tank production and was given a so-called critical defense status, meaning that his work was considered so vital to the war effort that he could not be drafted. He tried every possible means of getting out of the mill and into the war, but the authorities would not permit it. As more and more of his friends and relatives either volunteered or were drafted and headed off to their wartime military destinations, his frustration grew. But he could not change the minds of his superiors or of the recruiters for the various branches of the service.

After the war, he was haunted by the fact that he did not serve and no amount of rationalization about the critical importance of what he did do would assuage him. I should also mention that he did not finish high school, and he was also always acutely aware of that additional missing credential. Later, when he entered the business world and achieved some small measure of success, he was constantly reminded of the lack of an appropriate resume. He often remarked that whenever he entered a new business environment, the two questions he most frequently encountered were, "What did you do in the war?" and "Where did you go to college?" One of my earliest and most recurring memories of my dad is of him saying to me, "I don't care what career you choose, but you must go to college and you must serve your country." I heard this over and over again and, in truth, I don't think I ever had a negative response to his oft-stated feelings. Indeed, they became an integral part of my own value system. Bear in mind that not only was my father a high school dropout, but no one in our entire family had ever gone to college. When I did enroll at the University of Pittsburgh, he took considerable heat from our largely lower-class family, but not nearly as much as he did the following year when he allowed my sister, Beb, to matriculate at Duquesne University. He never flinched but rather insisted that his children were going to be educated at least through the college level. The same thing went for my younger brother, Jack, who also attended college and law school.

Four years later, having transferred from Pitt to LaSalle College in Philadelphia and completing my premed courses, I was accepted to medical school. I remember showing him the acceptance letter. I could tell from his rather understated response that he either did not understand or did not quite believe it was true. You must realize that there was no medical history of any kind in our family. Until that point, everyone was quite healthy. I don't recall ever being in a hospital and we did not have a family or primary care physician as is so common today. When my father did grasp the fact that I would be spending four more years in school, his first and, I think, his only question was to ask when I was going to find time to serve in the military. While assuring him that I would do so, I confess that, at the time, I had absolutely no idea how I would fulfill that family obligation. At that time I'm certain that I had no idea that a country called Vietnam even existed.

My knowledge of geopolitics did not increase over the next several years. I was totally immersed in my medical studies. In addition, I worked in the hospital lab at night to help defray some of my expenses. I was married with five kids and still had very little time to pay attention to the growing conflict in Vietnam. In retrospect, it may have been at least partially because my surgical residency was at the Hospital of the University of Pennsylvania, located in West Philadelphia, that my knowledge of and concern for that war increased exponentially in early 1967. The Penn campus was a hotbed of unrest and protest. Antiwar rallies and demonstrations were becoming increasingly common. As you might have guessed, I reacted as my father would have under the circumstances. I was anti the antiwar movement. Again, I emphasize that I had no particular knowledge of why we were fighting, no understanding of the threat of communism, and certainly no concept of where in the world Vietnam was located or why it was so important. All I knew was that we were at war and that our guys were being killed and wounded in significant numbers.

By mid-1967, the war was reaching a fever pitch, as were the protesters. Antiwar activity on Penn's campus was a constant and, for some, an all-consuming way of life. I instinctively regarded all the protesters as unthinking, unpatriotic, and unimportant. The truly important people for me were the young men who answered their country's call and were both fighting and dying in a distant land that few of the protesters could find on a map. My only thought was that I had acquired medical and surgical skills that could help those who were wounded in combat. I contacted the appropriate folks at the U.S. Naval Headquarters in Washington and indicated that if they would guarantee me a billet as a surgeon with the Marines, I would relinquish the deferment they had given to me to finish my residency training in surgery. After a bit of back-and-forth they agreed and I soon received my orders to report to Camp Lejeune, North Carolina, for the physician's version of basic training with the Marines.

For six weeks we did calisthenics, jogged, climbed rope ladders, and listened to an endless series of talks and lectures that proved ultimately to have absolutely nothing to do with taking care of casualties under combat conditions. I distinctly remember one gunnery sergeant telling us not to worry about our safety in the face of an attacking enemy force. He said that the Marines so loved and honored their doctors that every Marine would go down fighting before they would let any of them get to us. To me that simply meant that we would be the last to die.

I had some leave time after boot camp to say good-bye to family, and then the time came for me to go to Vietnam. My father took me to the airport and waited with me for the plane that would take me to my destination. He stood there beaming and when I asked him what was going on, he said not to worry. When the attendant called for first-class boarding, Dad nudged my arm and told me he had spoken with the TWA manager, who had cheerfully agreed to upgrade me to first class at no additional charge since I was going off to war. I don't think I appreciated at the time how much my father would participate vicariously in my Vietnam experience, although I remembered his frustration at being blocked out of World War II; I should have anticipated the intensity of his response.

The long flights to Guam and then Okinawa were uneventful. We were still in standard khaki dress uniforms. Actually, it was the only uniform I owned. On Okinawa, we were informed that these uniforms could not be worn "in country" and everyone was issued "jungle fatigues" and boots. I suppose it is safe to confess, at this point, I managed to hide in the john and avoid the gamma globulin injections that were required at that time. I can't quote a source, but I absolutely believed that there was no indication or proven benefit from these shots.

Before the day had ended, I was on a C-130 headed straight for Da Nang, Vietnam. I don't know exactly what I expected to find upon landing at the military airport just outside, but it certainly was not the plywood-floored tin hut that was the Da Nang terminal. It was nearly dark by the time we disembarked. I approached a small wooden makeshift desk manned by an Air Force sergeant and told him that I had orders to travel to Phu Bai. Pleasantly, but nonchalantly, he informed me that there would be no more flights that evening but if I checked back in the morning, he was certain they could put me on something going north. I asked what accommodations were available for the night. He said there was an officers' club a few miles down the road but he did not recommend walking there at night. When I asked where I could sleep nearby, fully expecting him to point out a building, he smiled pleasantly again and allowed as how I might find a comfortable patch of green grass somewhere outside the "terminal." Realizing that my choices were quite limited, I took his advice and carried my suitbag to what seemed like a soft green patch of grass very close to the cyclone fence surrounding the airfield. I saw two Marines carrying M16s and figured I was reasonably safe. Using my bag as a pillow, I fell into a deep sleep. I was exhausted from all that traveling, all those long miles from home. I know I was sound asleep because of the way in which I was awakened the following dawn. I can still hear the roar and feel the hot wind. I jumped up fast and ran a few yards for my life, only then turning around to see a big jet fighter, engine roaring, sitting about fifteen yards inside that cyclone fence with its big tail pointing directly at me. There was not another soul around with whom to share my fright and embarrassment. In the dark that night, I had unwittingly chosen to sleep directly under the tail of a fighter jet. All other alarm clocks before and since then have paled in comparison.

Chapter Three

Boot Camp

Back to Camp Lejeune and basic training: People are always amazed to learn that the Marines required their assigned Navy doctors to spend six weeks at a Marine base under the tutelage of one of their world-renowned drill sergeants. Truth be told, they were easy on us, at least as compared to the intense and extremely challenging ordeal of newly enlisted recruits. Our training, however, was not a total walk in the park.

There was one anesthesiologist in our group who was, charitably put, considerably overweight. I would guess that he carried about 260 pounds on a five-feet-one frame. He was also a cigarette smoker, and it was obvious from day one that he had virtually no exercise tolerance.

This in no way discouraged our drill sergeant, who pointed out that it was the responsibility of the group to see that he made it through the drills.

One of the obstacle courses we were required to cross contained a twelve-foot-high wall made of what appeared to be railroad ties. A mesh of thick bull rope was draped over the wooden wall. We were told that every man had to climb up one side of the obstacle, then down the other. Needless to say, our chubby buddy from anesthesia couldn't climb three rungs of the rope without becoming acutely short of breath. Our friendly drillmaster said in a somewhat firm way that no one was going home until we got this load up and over the wall. Four of us, two under each bulging thigh and butt cheek, hoisted this fat ass up, over, and down, resulting in five cases of shortness of breath instead of one.

I have always had mixed feelings about my time at Camp Lejeune. I certainly cannot claim that I learned anything that would eventually help me as a combat surgeon. The lectures on health and hygiene were dull and hopelessly outdated. There was virtually no information presented with reference to the actual care of the wounded and absolutely nothing about the logistics of moving casualties from the field of battle through triage, surgery, and the medevac system. In truth, my fondest memory of the entire basic training experience was a bus ride back from a training site during which a gunny sergeant sang all the lyrics to the raunchiest ballad I ever heard. It was called "the Ballad of Doty Rye." I would dearly love to find a copy of this stirring song or, better yet, hear someone sing it again. I doubt if, even by today's standards, it would be publishable in any respectable publication.

Chapter Four

Phu Bai and Ian

The C-123 rumbled down the runway. It seemed to be moving incredibly slowly, and I was absolutely convinced that it would never get off the ground. Eventually though, it did begin to lift off, but at what seemed to be an agonizingly slow rate. I was still not convinced that we would ever become airborne and began wondering just how much weight was inside the crates that were strapped to the floor in the center of the plane. Suddenly the afterburners kicked in and our ascent increased in both speed and lift angle. My confidence that I would actually get to my destination in Phu Bai was at least partially restored.

The small airfield at Phu Bai was approximately fifty to seventy-five yards from the main medical buildings. I remember walking past military ambulances, seemingly parked at random around the complex. The casualty volume at Phu Bai seemed like it would be relatively light from what I'd heard, but there were two events that happened while I was there that I will never forget.

During my first week at Phu Bai I had my first opportunity to triage and treat wounded Marines. The light volume of casualties gave me a good chance to become acclimated to what I thought at the time were combat surgical conditions. I, of course, had no notion of what was to come. There was a day when we did receive more than the usual number of wounded so that for a time all of our surgeons and corpsmen were quite busy attending to their respective casualties.

As the triage surgeon, I supervised the evaluation of the groups of injured grunts and designated their treatment. The more seriously wounded were sent directly to one of the operating rooms for definitive repair of injured parts. The less seriously wounded were sent to the minor surgical area for debridement of smaller wounds. Just as I finished arranging for the disposition of what I thought was the last of the injured men, litter bearers came through the door with an ARVN (Army of the Republic of Vietnam) soldier who had been shot in the right arm. It was a through and through wound that had severed the brachial artery and shattered the elbow joint. Someone had applied a makeshift tourniquet around the mid-biceps area. I could not be certain if there was any nerve damage, but I knew that if we could not restore blood flow to his arm and hand, he would probably lose the entire forearm. I sent him back to the remaining open operating room and was looking around for someone to assist me at surgery when an Army captain in very spiffy, well-pressed jungle fatigues walked into the triage area. I could not believe my eyes. It was Ian Forest, whom I knew from the Hospital of the University of Pennsylvania (HUP), where he had been training in internal medicine while I was doing my surgical residency. "What the hell are you doing here, Ian?" I asked, absolutely astonished to see him again, especially under these circumstances. He explained that he was assigned to an Army unit near Saigon where some of his unit were sent to examine a radio installation. I never asked what that meant and to this day I still do not know why they were there. What I did know was that I needed help in the operating room and that Ian was eager to help.

We got him in a scrub suit and he spent the next hour or so assisting me while I debrided the wound of this unfortunate

ARVN soldier and repaired his brachial artery. I still remember how pleased we both were to see the ARVN's pink hand and to feel a good pulse at the wrist.

Ian left immediately after the procedure to join his team on their inspection trip. I didn't see him again until we both returned to HUP two years later to complete our respective training programs. By that time he had switched from internal medicine to urology. Not long after we returned, we were both asked to speak at the University's Women's Association. The women were amazed and understandably confused by our very different presentations. I spoke of the efficient system in place to care for the wounded, emphasizing the prioritization of all equipment and supplies for combat troops. I described rather gently but truthfully the constant danger from incoming enemy fire. My entire presentation dealt with the cold reality of war. I showed a few slides depicting wounds but kept things on the mild side. Ian, on the other hand, dealt with Army life around Saigon. At that time, there was minimal danger of enemy attack, and most doctors and medics were involved in sick call and community outreach programs for the Vietnamese in the area. During the question-and-answer period, one of the ladies asked about drug use by the troops, a topic getting a lot of press in the United States. To my amazement, Ian said that heavy use of drugs by troops in the Saigon area was quite common with marijuana by far the most frequently abused substance.

I could only remember one instance during my entire tour of duty in which drugs were even mentioned. It had happened at the Dong Ha combat base. We received a large number of casualties from a sweep that was underway just to the south of where we were stationed. As always, the more seriously wounded Marines were on litters suspended on iron horses in the triage building. The routine always included stripping the man naked so as to allow careful assessment of the entire body so that no wound, however small, would be missed. Any personal items carried by the Marine—cigarettes, keys, pictures, wallets, etc.— were placed in a small canvas "ditty" bag and attached to the man's litter. On one occasion, and one only, during my entire year, someone let out a very loud "Oh boy" and held up a small bag of what was determined to be marijuana. It was immediately discarded without further comment. At no other time did I ever witness or suspect the presence or use of any illegal substance. The obvious dichotomy, I think, points to an aspect of the war in Vietnam that I think caused some of the confusion that existed in the minds of those who relied on the media for their information. Depending on where the reporter was assigned, an entirely different scenario would be described.

Chapter Five

Fido Mignon

The Dong Ha Combat base became the headquarters of the Third Marine Division in October of 1967. Delta Med (D Med) was the medical facility on that base staffed by Navy physicians and corpsmen. I was one of the Navy surgeons assigned there from October through December of 1967. We cared for casualties from the US Marine Corps, the ARVN, prisoners from the Vietcong and North Vietnamese Army (NVA) regulars, and occasionally, civilians.

The Marines were always interested in talking to any wounded prisoners. For that reason, we always had a Marine officer with us who was reasonably fluent in the Vietnamese language. Captain Mike Hansen (not his real name) was the most memorable of these linguistic specialists, not only because he also spoke Swahili, but because he offered to give lessons in Vietnamese to any of us who were interested. I sat in on two sessions, knowing full well that I was devoid of linguistic talent. Those who persisted were rewarded a few weeks later when Captain Mike told the class that they were all invited into the village of Dong Ha to have dinner with the mayor and his family. As a former class member, I was also extended an invitation but since I was the first-call surgeon the evening of the dinner, I was unable to attend.

Six of our men went into the village, enjoyed dinner and Vietnamese conversation with the mayor and his family, and then returned home to the base. The next day all six were in our hospital with fever, diarrhea, and crampy abdominal pain. They were treated with intravenous fluids, antibiotics, and painkillers, and thankfully, all recovered within a few days. The true cause of their agony could not be discovered since laboratory testing was extremely limited on a combat base. However, one of the internists, with the help our interpreter captain, returned to the village and diplomatically questioned the mayor about the party menu. He enthusiastically explained to them that the meal consisted of rice, vegetables, noodles, in addition to the main entrée, dog!

From that day on, whenever one of the six "victims" walked into the chow tent, all of us would begin irreverently barking and howling.

Chapter Six

ARVN vs. NVA

The first time I had the opportunity to evaluate and treat wounded soldiers from the Army of the Republic of Vietnam (ARVN), I learned a lesson about pain tolerance. Six ARVNs were brought into triage screaming "Dow, dow, dow," the Vietnamese word for pain, and the only thing we could discern amidst their collective yelling. The team quickly stripped them naked, looking for what I was certain would be major, serious wounds. Instead, we found small superficial shrapnel wounds that we usually referred to as "dings." Only their extremities were involved. None of them had any major wounds of the chest, abdomen, or head. Each of these tiny injuries was cleaned and bandaged amidst repeated outcries of "dow, dow, dow." We finished their units. The noise level then increased exponentially. I told the interpreter to explain to them that their wounds were quite minor and that they had to leave to make way for more casualties, hoping that the thought of other wounded on their way to us would motivate them to move. The scene that followed can only be described as comical, something out of a B movie. Those with minor leg wounds tried to stand but quickly sagged to the floor. After being helped to a standing position, they left triage limping profoundly. Those with superficial upper extremity wounds used their "good" arms to support their bad arms and left the area listing badly to the injured side. It was really very hard not to laugh as the last of them went out the door. I don't think anyone could imagine their performance in combat conditions.

A few days later, three badly wounded North Vietnamese Army (NVA) regulars were stretchered into triage under heavy guard. Not a sound emanated from any of them. Examination revealed that one soldier had his right arm nearly severed at the mid-biceps level. Another had multiple penetrating wounds of the abdomen with parts of his small intestine extruding through one of his wounds. The third soldier had abdominal and chest wounds that required immediate placement of a tube into his chest to drain blood. All three of them required immediate major surgery. While in triage, the three NVA remained absolutely stoic, making no sound when moved to the operating room prior to the induction of anesthesia. Postoperatively, they remained quiet, giving no indication that they were in any way in pain or in need of medication to alleviate it.

These three were medevaced shortly thereafter, leaving me with the rather distinct impression that we had perhaps backed the wrong side. I certainly didn't think I wanted to share a foxhole with an ARVN soldier, but I was even more certain that I didn't want to encounter an NVA regular in a dark alley.

Chapter Seven

Scrotal Surgeon

Land mines are a fact of life in any combat zone. Tripping one can be instantly fatal in many cases or, if not, can result in devastating injuries to the entirety of the lower extremities. Everyone has seen media coverage of returning veterans who have lost part or all of one or both their legs. These are indeed sad cases to see, but we know from experience that careful surgery and intensive rehabilitation, including the use of modern prosthetic devices, can allow many of these men and women to return to active and productive lives.

Less well known, however, and certainly far less discussed, and much less publicized, are the serious wounds to the anus, penis, and scrotum that can be caused by the upward explosion of a mine. Nothing can really prepare you for your first exposure to a nineteen-year-old Marine who has stepped on a land mine and arrives in triage where examination of his wounds indicates severe damage to his feet, legs, and thighs. (Frequently, an extremity is simply missing and presumably blown off by the force of the explosion). He also has missing testicles, multiple lacerations of the scrotal sac, and wounds of the penis. I think I had some sort of deep spiritual, primal response to these genital injuries. Maybe it was just a "guy thing," but the realization that this young boy would never know sexual pleasure and would never father his own child, filled me with a great sadness.

I would take these kids to the operating room and work diligently, maybe even zealously, to try to reconstruct any remnant of manhood for them. I feel like it was the least I could do and certainly what I would hope a surgeon would do for me. Later, while completing my active duty time at the Philadelphia Naval Hospital, I did see a few amputees who, although missing testicles, had undergone plastic surgery during which a skin tube was created to give the appearance of a penis. While not functional, it at least provided the man with some psychological boost.

You never hear about the young men who are wounded in this fashion. I wonder if there is any veteran's benefit available that could even come close to compensating these guys for their loss.

Chapter Eight

Lopez

I wouldn't blame anyone for challenging my memory of what happened in Vietnam forty years ago. I wonder sometimes just how accurate my recollections are, but when I tell the story of Lopez, I assure you that facts are not only accurate but unforgettable.

I was the triage surgeon on duty at the Dong Ha combat base when we received word via radio that a large number of casualties were on their way to us. One of the helicopter crew usually gave us three numbers—for example, seventeen, thirteen, four—over the radio. We could then know what to prepare for—seventeen walking wounded, thirteen litter wounded, four KIAs (killed in action). Those designated as walking wounded would usually require simpler procedures such as debridements (manually cleaning wounds with scissors and scalpels), stitching, the use of small splints, or anything on a low level of wound care. Those on litters were generally more seriously wounded and frequently required more complex surgery in the operating room for injuries such as gunshot wounds to the abdomen and massive extremity wounds.

The KIAs were taken from the chopper directly to a place called Graves Registration, which was usually situated on the opposite side of the helo pad and well away from the triage area. A contingent of Marines was assigned to Graves Registration; their job was to attempt to properly identify the bodies. They would then place each of the bodies into a body bag in preparation for immediate flight to a military mortuary away from the war zone.

Try to picture now this entire scene. Two helicopters, one a CH-46 Sea Knight, the other a CH-53 Sea Stallion or Jolly Green Giant, land simultaneously in front of the large triage building at the Dong Ha combat base. The four soldiers who died in action are taken to Graves Registration. The fourteen litters containing the most seriously wounded are placed on supporting iron horses. Standing at the doorway entrance to triage (the French word for sorting out), I make a quick appraisal of each litter and try to have the worst of the badly wounded placed in the first position with the rest roughly placed according to injury severity based on that first quick look. You would be surprised at the accuracy of that initial once-over in placing the men in reasonable order for evaluation and treatment.

Lopez was one of those Marines whose wounds were so severe that he was placed in the first slot, where my team began our oft-repeated and extremely efficient initial assessment. It was obvious that he was in profound shock from extreme blood loss. He had no obtainable blood pressure. I was certain I could feel a pulse. He was extremely pale and cold. The anesthesiologist assigned to the station immediately put a tube into his lungs so that respirations could begin manually. The team stripped him naked, which was standard procedure, so that every inch of his body could be checked for injuries. Lopez had multiple wounds to his abdomen, chest, and all four of his extremities. Remarkably, there were no head or face wounds. Even as this rapid assessment was taking place, I asked the corpsman to open the chest kit, which was nothing more than a scalpel and a rib retractor. God bless the corpsman. He actually had it in his hand before I even asked. Another corpsman confirmed that the Marine had no obtainable blood pressure. I quickly opened Lopez's left chest with the scalpel, put the rib retractor in place, opened the pericardium (heart sac), and began directly massaging his heart with my gloved hand.

A large tube was inserted into his right chest cavity in order to drain any blood that may have been accumulating there. While I continued to massage his heart, the anesthesiologist continued to breathe for him while other team members assessed and dressed his wounds. Large-bore intravenous lines were already in place, and blood was being pumped in as rapidly as possible. In spite of this Herculean effort, we were unable to restore any hint of a pulse or blood pressure. Reluctantly, I pronounced Lopez dead and told the litter bearers to take him to Graves Registration.

Moments later, the stretcher bearers came charging back into triage with Lopez still on the litter, swearing that he was moving. They insisted on a reassessment of his condition. Once again, I placed him in the number-one slot and once again the team carried out a full resuscitative effort. Again, there was no pulse or blood pressure to be obtained, and I had little choice except to once again pronounce poor Lopez dead.

Approximately ten minutes elapsed before four guys from Graves Registration came charging back into triage carrying Lopez. This time they were frightened and very angry. "This sonovabitch is moving," they screamed. "We're not taking him back!" For the third time, I placed him at a station. By now, the whole scene was attracting a lot of attention. We redid the entire effort with the same result. I was, however, not about to send him back to Graves for the third time, so I called one of the other surgeons over and asked him to assess the situation. He did and said, "Jim, he's dead, there's nothing we can do for him."

At this point, I had to tell him that I knew he was dead but I couldn't sent him back to Graves Registration without having the Marines go crazy, so I told him to take Lopez to the operating room for surgery. "What the hell do you want me to operate on?" he asked me. I told him to open Lopez's belly to see what was going on, to just do it.

Sometime later, after I had triaged all of the other casualties that had come in with Lopez, I went back to the operating room to see how things were going. The anesthesiologist informed me that shortly after the surgery on Lopez began, a tracing began to appear on the EKG screen, first very slowly and a bit irregularly, then a little faster and quite regularly. We did not have the advantage of direct arterial line monitoring in that situation but relied solely on the blood pressure cuff to detect any presence of a vital sign. The anesthesiologist indicated that, in spite of repeated attempts, he had not been able to hear a blood pressure with that cuff.

I continued to watch the surgery. There were multiple shrapnel holes in his small and large intestines that required repair. One section of his colon was so damaged that it had to be completely removed. About twenty or thirty minutes later, the anesthesiologist excitedly exclaimed that he thought he was in fact hearing a blood pressure at about sixty over palpation, meaning that he could hear the systolic number but not the diastolic value. He continued pumping blood and fluids into Lopez and a few moments later said that he was clearly hearing something at about 80/50. That, as you can well imagine, literally lifted the spirits of everyone in the room. By the time the abdominal portion of the procedure was over, Lopez' blood pressure was over 100 systolic and he was actually requiring the use of anesthetic medication to keep him asleep and comfortable. I scrubbed in to the surgery at that point to close the left chest incision that I had created earlier for the open cardiac massage. Lopez was then transferred to the intensive care unit (ICU). He was in critical condition but was maintaining a good pulse and blood pressure on his own.

The amazing conclusion to this story occurred the next morning when we arrived in the intensive care unit to make postoperative rounds. Not only was Lopez awake, but his breathing tube had been removed and he was breathing comfortably on his own. The next day he was stable enough to be medevaced to Da Nang. I never saw him again.

The story of Lopez is the stuff of which legends are made. Everyone at the Dong Ha combat base was aware of what transpired. The good feeling that permeated the base could not compare with the sense of accomplishment felt by the corpsmen, physicians, and surgeons of the Third Medical Battalion, and especially by those of us who actually provided his care. For me, it was a profound lesson in humility and a powerful reminder that we do not have all the answers. I know that by all measurable criteria, Lopez was dead. I know the well-trained, experienced combat surgical team assessed him not once or twice but three times, each time finding no evidence of life. I freely admit that I ordered him to surgery on a purely instinctual, emotional basis. I do not know how or why he survived. I do know that no matter how advanced our training, no matter how sophisticated our technology, no matter how aggressive our effort, the mystery of life, the will to live, and the power of the spirit will always be one step ahead of us- with Lopez.

Chapter Nine

I'll Take That Gun, Doc

The advance headquarters of the Third Marine Division moved north from Phu Bai in October of 1968. The medical facility there was designated Delta Med. The medical staff was made up of two orthopedic surgeons, four general surgeons (including yours truly) four anesthesiologists, a couple of internists, and about two dozen hospital corpsmen. All were, of course, U.S. Navy personnel assigned to the Marine Corps. We did not have a neurosurgeon or an ophthalmologist, so that serious head or eye injuries were stabilized and then choppered to one of the hospital ships cruising out in the Da Nang Bay, the *Sanctuary* or the *Repose*, neither of which was designed as a hospital ship. They were converted freighters with small helipads affixed to their sterns—emphasis on the word *small.* Many of the more severe head injuries required one or more physicians to accompany them on the flight in order to assist with breathing using an endotracheal tube(a breathing tube in the windpipe), occasionally to carry out cardiac massage, and sometimes just to keep pressure on a bleeding wound.

I flew quite a few of those missions accompanying a wounded Marine, and after landing on the deck, I gave a report to the onboard surgeon who would then assume his care. Most often, we reboarded the helicopter and returned immediately to Delta Med. Occasionally, we were forced to stay on the ship if the chopper crew received orders diverting them to another mission.

The first time I was required to stay behind, I was at a bit of a loss as to what to do until the helicopter returned to pick me up. I had never been on a ship before, having come from my home in Philadelphia to Camp Lejuene for basic training with the Marines and then straight to Vietnam. I knew absolutely nothing about the U.S. Navy or its rules, regulations, and traditions. A young petty officer told me that I was welcome to come aboard and wait in the wardroom. I thanked him and started to enter the ship through one of those large heavy doors when an ensign appeared in front of me and informed me that I could not enter the ship while wearing my .45 pistol on my hip.

His exact words were, "I'll take your gun." Instantly recalling all my Marine Corps basic training emphasizing again and again that a Marine never, ever surrenders his weapon, I said to this poor kid, "You've got a better chance of getting pregnant than getting my gun" (I always loved that line). He was a bit taken aback and called the lieutenant commander, who arrived in seconds and gently promised me that he would assume personal responsibility for my weapon and return it to me prior to my take-off back to Delta Med.

Reluctantly I did part with my gun and followed him to the wardroom for a cup of coffee. In retrospect, I imagine he had encountered this situation before with other armed visitors.

Chapter Ten

Not Quite "*M*A*S*H*"

Whenever people learn of my experience as a combat surgeon with the Marines in Vietnam, and, especially if they hear of my function as the commanding officer of a Navy surgical team in Khe Sanh during the three-month siege of the now famous combat base, the first thing I'm asked is if it was like the popular television show *M*A*S*H*. My response is always the same. Yes, it was sort of like *M*A*S*H* except there were no women! That TV series was so widely watched that virtually everyone was conditioned to think that all combat surgical teams had a collection of young, beautiful nurses to assist them. A little-known fact is that the Marines did not allow females in their combat theaters of operation—at least that's what I was told in 1968. Our medical team consisted of Navy physicians, Navy corpsmen, and Navy male nurses. This all-male environment lent itself nicely to a version of the English language that outsiders, especially the ladies, might find offensive.

In early November of 1967 we were informed that elements of the U.S. Army would be conducting a major sweep (search and destroy) very near the Dong Ha Combat base, which was, of course, the headquarters of the Third Marine Division. We were asked if we could assist in the care of their casualties and, specifically, if the wounded could be medevaced from the field to our triage/surgical facility. Naturally we responded affirmatively. Within hours, a female Army nurse colonel arrived and informed us that a group of Army female nurses would be assigned to Delta Med to help in the care of Army casualties. I remember trying to explain to the colonel that while we were indeed grateful for the offer, we were somewhat concerned about exposing her nurse officers to recently wounded U.S. Marines who tended to use rather "colorful" language as part of routine communication. Another point was that because of the severity of injuries and the types of treatments given, the soldiers were always in their beds completely naked with maybe just a sheet over them. The colonel was unfazed and assured me that her girls could handle the situation.

You probably don't need me to tell you what happened next. The Army began its major sweep just to our south while the Marines continued their combat operations to our north and west. We soon had a mixture of casualties from both areas in our ICU and on our wards.

Early in the first morning, after all the action began, we started making rounds in the ICU. The twenty beds were filled with postoperative wounded from the Army and Marine Corps. The Army nurses accompanied us on these rounds. I was walking on eggshells and breathing rather shallowly, knowing we were skating on thin ice. After examining a few of the soldiers, we approached the bed of a young Marine who had sustained abdominal and chest injuries and who had undergone major surgery late the night before. He was awake and stable. While we were looking him over, one of the Army nurses took his hand and told him that he was doing fine and that everything would be all right, to which the Marine responded, "Everything would be perfect if you would suck my dick."

Surely you must know how difficult it is to discipline a seriously wounded man. It is highly unlikely that you can come up with a sanction or punishment that will faze him in the slightest: "What're ya gonna do—cut my hair and send me to Vietnam?" There was a pregnant pause, someone told the Marine to pipe down, and we moved to the next bed.

The next day the Army nurses were gone, the colonel having announced that the major part of the Army action was over and that the nurses were being moved to where they were needed more.

Chapter Eleven

Dr. Terry Andrews—A Good Decision Maker

The triage facility at Dong Ha was quite large, measuring about one hundred feet square. It was the basic Southeast Asian construction—plywood sides and a tin roof. In front of this building, facing north, was a thirty-foot pole flying the American flag. It took a while for our fearless leaders to recognize that the NVA forward artillery observers were using the flag as a distance marker for their artillery and rockets, but after a few hits on the medical complex, the flag was discreetly lowered and stored away for future use.

Incoming rounds were fairly common at Dong Ha and so the Seabees, the Navy construction teams, were prevailed upon to build a steel revetment in front of the triage building in the hope that exploding artillery lobbed in from our northern neighbors would not send a hail of shrapnel through the triage area, especially while we were treating casualties. It was, indeed, effective except for those shells that were fired over the revetment and landed in the Delta Med complex. One such round, although very serious, still makes me laugh when I think about it.

Dr. Terry Andrews was an internist from San Francisco assigned to our battalion. He was always pleasant, upbeat, and comical in a cynical sort of way. Because of his specialty, he did more sick call than casualty care but was always ready and willing to help out with the wounded.

When we first arrived at the combat base, the men's' room or "shitter" was the classic "four-holer" where four men, regardless of name, rank, or serial number, could sit side by side and enjoy the camaraderie afforded by simultaneous movements. After all, aren't all men the same with their pants down? These colonic collectives are part of military lore and are fondly remembered by all who utilized these perfectly practical poopers. They did, however cause a deep yearning for a classic porcelain toilet on which one could sit as if on a real throne, enjoy some degree of comfort, and ponder the tactical situation surrounding one's current effort.

Imagine the surprise and delight when the Seabees installed a beautiful new real live white flushable toilet. It was upon this throne of glory that the good Dr. Andrews was sitting (and no doubt pondering) when we began taking heavier-than-usual incoming artillery and rocket fire.

As Terry tells the story, he was literally caught between "a shit and a sweat." He was ever so reluctant to give up his time on the only flush toilet in the entire battalion—there was always a line to use it—but realized his extreme vulnerability in this exposed position. He does not recall how long he debated with himself, but after hearing a nearby explosion, he hoisted his drawers and leapt across the catwalk into a nearby bunker. Almost simultaneously, that gorgeous porcelain shitter took a direct hit from an 88mm rocket and was literally blown to kingdom come. Not much of Terry would have been found had he not listened to his survival instincts, although he did insist that he would have died a happy man.

Chapter Twelve

Holes in the Fuselage

Recently my wife, my daughter, and I spent part of our summer vacation on a tour of the Grand Canyon National Park in Arizona and also of Bryce Canyon National Park in Utah. Since the exchange rate for the euro was so ridiculous, we thought it was time to see the beauty of some of our own country.

One of the optional add-on attractions of the Grand Canyon phase of the trip was the opportunity to take a helicopter ride around the rim of the canyon. We bravely purchased three tickets from the tour guide but at flight time, our daughter decided that she would rather forego the pleasure and stay on solid ground. Ever the true gentleman and loving father, I told my wife to go on without us, which she in fact did. I would gladly stay with Caitlin and do a walking appraisal of this breathtaking natural wonder. As we did our exploring, Caitlin expressed a bit of the "guilts" and apologized for keeping me from the ride. "Believe me," I told her, "my helicopter memories are very unpleasant and I really don't need that experience right now." I told her that she was actually doing me a favor by giving me an excuse to stay on terra firma with her. She knew that I had served in Vietnam but had never heard any of my chopper stories.

My first helicopter ride naturally took place on a pitch-black night when you couldn't even see your hand in front of your face. I was the triage surgeon on first call at the Third Medical Battalion facility at the Dong Ha combat base. It was just after midnight when I was notified that a recon patrol had been ambushed and two choppers were on their way to us carrying multiple casualties.

Triage is the French word for "sort out," and indeed, my first job was to rapidly assess the wounded as they entered and then prioritize treatment based on injury severity. One young

Marine was pale white, cold, and in shock. As the team was stripping him naked and inserting large intravenous lines in him, I quickly observed and palpated nearly every inch of his body surface. He did not seem to have any wounds of his chest, abdomen, arms or legs, but I knew there had to be a wound somewhere to account for the absence of a measurable blood pressure. Palpating his scalp, I found a small hole just behind his lower left ear. As he began to respond to intravenous fluids, blood began to spurt from the hole. I was pretty certain that his carotid artery had been hit by a piece of shrapnel and that he could bleed to death from his wound. I say a shrapnel wound rather than a bullet because a bullet in this area would most likely have resulted in instant death for him.

At the Dong Ha combat base medical facility (Delta Med), we had general surgeons, orthopedic surgeons, anesthesiologists, Navy hospital corpsmen, and all the equipment and supplies one would ever need to accomplish almost every kind of combat surgery. However, because head and eye injuries requiring immediate surgery were relatively unusual, the neurosurgeons and ophthalmologists were stationed on the hospital ships, the *Sanctuary* and the *Repose*, which were on station in Da Nang

Bay, several miles off the coast and presumably out of artillery range. I had my index finger in the hole behind his ear to stop further bleeding. I knew immediately that this Marine was going to require the services of a neurosurgeon to remove some of his skull bone in order to get to the area of the carotid artery injury. With my finger in the dike, and his blood pressure responding to intravenous fluids and blood transfusions, I called for a chopper to take him to the hospital ship. I had good control of the wound with my finger and rather than waste time by trying to find someone to replace me, I decided to fly with him. The anesthesiologist, who inserted the breathing tube and was controlling his respirations, was also coming along.

Within minutes, a twin-rotor CH-46 Sea Knight helicopter arrived and lowered its rear hydraulic gate for us to board. We boarded carefully with our very fragile cargo and flew off into the blackest night I have ever known. You must understand that in this northernmost portion of South Vietnam, there was no electricity. Add to that, dense cloud cover with no moon or stars, and you have the very definition of blackness or the complete absence of light.

The chopper pilot flew us through this soup trying to

find the hospital ship. I haven't a clue how he found it, but after about fifteen minutes in the air, one of the door gunners pointed downward indicating, I was hoping, that we had found the *Repose* and were about to land. The *Repose* and the *Sanctuary* were relatively tiny vessels compared to such big monsters as the destroyers, battleships, or carriers. The helodecks were barely big enough to hold a CH-46. As the deck officer was guiding us in through the blackness, he apparently decided that our approach was less than perfect and waved the pilot off. I learned that the deck officer has total command of any craft attempting to land on his ship. His word is law. Our pilot pulled up on the joystick and, as expected, the front of the chopper lifted higher than the rear causing Ben, our anesthesiologist, to almost fall off the hydraulic gate, which had been lowered as we were about to touch down. He was wearing a helmet and flak jacket and would have disappeared into the blackness of Da Nang Bay had he fallen off. He quickly got his bearings and scampered back onto the chopper. I irreverently started to laugh. I saw Ben at the fortieth reunion of the Third Medical Battalion and, needless to say, we relived that wild and crazy night.

Our injured Marine was taken directly to the operating

room and not only survived the surgery, but had no permanent brain damage. Usually, I would not be able to provide this kind of follow-up information, but the helicopter took off as soon as we offloaded our casualty and we had to stay aboard the ship until it returned in the morning.

Very early the very next day another CH-46 came out to the hospital ship. We jumped on and were quickly airborne and heading back to "D" Med. The flight path was over the Cua Viet River. All of the sudden, the door gunners began blasting away with their .50-caliber machine guns. The noise of the helicopter's motor was so loud that I couldn't hear the guns firing. I was watching the gunners and wondering what the hell they were doing, when one of them, who must have been reading my mind, pointed to the floor of the chopper where several three-quarter-inch holes were visible. I immediately understood that we were taking some ground fire. My only thought was to make myself very small and as inconspicuous as possible. Fortunately, no one was injured on that ride back and we were able to land safely at Dong Ha.

I took many other helicopter rides during my tour in Vietnam. Since then I have never looked upon them as my preferred mode of transportation, even though I will never be able to say enough about the courage and skill of the helicopter crews who did so much for both us and our patients during that difficult year. So, while my wife was circling the Grand Canyon with her tour group, listening to Jim Morrison sing "Riders on the Storm" through her earphones, I explained this entire story to my daughter. She was, as all kids can be, very wise and understanding of her dad's feelings about helicopter rides. "Don't worry," she said, "if it's a choice between being up there in one of those dumb little choppers or being here on solid ground with you, Dad, you win every time."

Chapter Thirteen

Dental Stories

I don't think much has been written about the dentists who served in the combat areas, but I can tell you three stories, one funny, two sad, about dentists who served with the Third Marine division in Vietnam.

The first is about Sam Harbison, a dentist and navy commander, who arrived at the Dong Ha combat base in October of 1968. He brought with him a team of dental techs and during regular clinic hours every day would see any Navy or Marine personnel in the area. I had been wearing a partial upper denture since the age of thirteen when I was involved in an accident while playing a game with my buddies. This resulted in breakage of several of my front teeth. My dad was the drinking buddy of a dentist who went to dental school at the turn of the twentieth century. This wonderful gentleman pulled several of my front teeth and provided me with a set of false teeth to fill the gap. I, of course, didn't know any better and simply accepted things as a matter of course.

Fifteen years later, enter Dr. Harbison and his team. I can still remember sitting in the chair at the base, my mouth wide open, the denture out, listening to Sam and his group enjoying a good laugh at my expense. When I asked what was so funny, Sam apologized but explained that the denture I had been wearing for fifteen years was in fact, a temporary prosthesis and should have been replaced with a permanent bridge shortly after it was put in. Dental humor.

The following year, when I was home in the states, Sam provided me with the appropriate mouthware while we were both at the Philadelphia Naval Hospital. God bless you Sam, wherever you are!

The second tale about a dentist is a kind of sad-happy mix. It was not unusual for any new arrival to our area to hop a ride on a helicopter heading for one of the hospital ships, the *Sanctuary* or the *Repose,* to visit the ship's store, where things like cameras and other goods could be purchased at deep discounts. A young dentist who was "in country" for only a few days took such a ride to purchase a camera and was flying back to our base when the chopper began to take ground fire. Military helicopters are not soundproofed and the noise level inside them when they are airborne is almost intolerable. The only way to know that the ship is being hit is to see the holes suddenly appear in the fuselage. It's a scary feeling. One such round came up through the bottom of the dentist's helicopter and passed through his left thigh, fracturing his femur but sparing the nerves and blood vessels. Because rehabilitation time for this injury is so long, it resulted in him being evacuated back to the United States immediately after surgery to have the wound cleaned and the fractured bone stabilized. And so, three days after arriving in the Republic of Vietnam, our "tooth-puller" was on his way home with his camera and his Purple Heart.

The third story is the saddest of the three. A newly arrived dental technician had mistakenly gone to the headquarters of the Third Marine Division to report for duty. He was told there that he was in the wrong area and needed to go about a half mile down a dirt road to Delta Med where he could report to his commanding officer. They very kindly provided a jeep and a driver to bring him to us. Just as the jeep exited Marine headquarters and started down the road to us, we began taking incoming artillery fire. The jeep, completely unprotected, made it about halfway down the road. We all began yelling and waving, trying to get the driver's attention to tell him to get off the road to take cover. I know he couldn't hear us and I guess he didn't see us because a few seconds later, the jeep took a direct hit from an incoming round. Both men were killed instantly.

A dentist and a dental tech, one seriously wounded, one killed, both serving their country during wartime. I'd be willing to bet they were both volunteers. Maybe you'll think of these stories the next time you're in the dentist's chair.

Chapter Fourteen

Graves Registration

I have thought long and hard about describing the scene in Graves Registration. As I mentioned elsewhere, the last thing I want to do is cause any pain for any relative or friend of a Marine who was killed in action. On the other hand, having seen this human devastation, I can only hope and pray that these memories, which stayed with me these many years, will provide others with a glimpse of the true horror of war and perhaps, in a small way, help lead us to a time when such human destruction will no longer be necessary or tolerated. My first impression of the inside of the Graves Registration building was that it was a holy and sacred place. The Marines assigned to work there moved quietly, almost softly, carefully searching for identification of the bodies. If it was necessary to move all or part of a body, it was done with a level of care bordering on reverential. Many of the Graves team were combat veterans and knew firsthand just what these dead heroes had been through. They also knew, as I did, that my presence there was completely superfluous. But they knew the "Lopez" story and were kindly tolerant as I went about my assigned task.

As I write this, I am trying to work up the courage to describe some of what I saw. The one KIA who always sticks in my mind (perhaps because I'm a thoracic surgeon) was a very young Marine whose face, head, arms, legs, and abdomen were completely intact, but whose ribs, breastbone, heart, and lungs were completely gone. The very minor solace was that he obviously died instantly and never knew what hit him.

Headless corpses were not uncommon, an indication, I think, of the tremendous velocity of the missiles that struck them. That's a concept and an experience that eludes civilians, including civilian surgeons. The damage to bones, muscles, and body organs from bullets and shrapnel is proportional to the size and speed with which the offending missile is moving. Remember that a civilian police .38 revolver has a muzzle velocity of about 930 feet/second. The M16 has a muzzle velocity of about 3,250 feet/second. If you recall $E=mc^2$ and think of E as body damage, you can begin to appreciate what the square of the muzzle velocity contributes to organ damage in the human body.

My most haunting memory is of a Marine whose entire body from the neck down was completely intact, but the skin of his face and head was flat on the floor. His skull and brains had been completely removed from his head, probably by a very high velocity piece of artillery shrapnel. It looked almost like a child's drawing of a man in the moon, a skin pancake with facial features.

Chapter Fifteen

Missing Pieces

An empty rib cage

A face without a skull

Bodies with no arms, no legs

O brave young Marine

Who stole your heart, your mind?

Who wrote your name on that shell?

Who set that mine in your path?

I want so badly to put you back together

But I cannot

I worry that you will arrive at the

Gates of Heaven with missing pieces,

But I believe with all my heart

That God will make you whole again.

I have to believe that

James O. Finnegan, MD
Former Commanding Officer
Charlie Med
Khe Sanh

Chapter Sixteen

Triage at Khe Sanh

Military historians say the siege lasted seventy-seven days. I could never figure out how they judged when it officially ended and how they were able to pick the exact number of days as seventy-seven. It is quite common for troops in a war zone to keep track of the number of days until their tour ends and they leave a hostile area for the safety of home. During the battle of Khe Sanh, our major concern was not counting days but staying alive on a day-by-day basis. The Navy doctors and corpsmen who took care of the wounded U.S. Marines during the now famous siege of Khe Sanh look back on it as a watershed moment in their lives. Few, if any, of us had ever heard of this tiny plateau located in the far northwest corner of Vietnam, but the experience of caring for so many wounded Marines under such adverse tactical circumstances on the red clay plateau has forever marked our souls and created bonds that few will ever know or understand.

Marine intelligence estimated incoming mortar, rocket, and artillery fire to be up to three thousand rounds per day, accounting for the fact that over 95 percent of the casualties we cared for had multiple shrapnel wounds, mostly of their extremities and abdomen.

During the cooler months of January and February, when a Marine was more likely to wear his helmet and button his protective flak jacket, the incidence of serious head and chest wounds was relatively low. Later, as the weather grew warmer and the tendency to shed these lifesaving accoutrements increased, so did the incidence of major upper body wounds.

As I write this in January 2008, I realize that it has been forty years since the beginning of the siege. It is still crystal clear in my mind. Dr. Ed Feldman is standing over a badly wounded Marine giving orders to the corpsman while stripping the casualty and examining every square inch of his body for wounds. One of the earliest lessons learned in the assessment of these combat injuries is that high-velocity explosions can injure even the most inaccessible parts of the human body. "Armpits and assholes" were checked on every casualty on a stretcher. As always, Eddie is calm, cool, and collected. No amount of incoming artillery, rocket, or mortar fire disturbs his demeanor. He will ultimately become a very successful obstetrician in Los Angeles, and the mothers he attends will never know that the guy who delivered their precious babies is a bona fide war hero.

The Marine on the next stretcher is badly wounded and Dr. Don Magilligan is inserting a tube into his left chest to drain blood and hopefully re-expand the lung. Dr. Joe Wolfe is at the head of the litter preparing to insert a breathing tube. Our corpsmen worked tirelessly alongside the physicians starting intravenous lines, applying dressings and splints, all the while keeping up a casual but reassuring banter with the injured grunts.

This scene repeated itself daily, sometimes hourly, during the long siege of the Khe Sanh combat base from January through March of 1968. The inflow of seriously wounded men varied from a few per hour up to sixty in a fifteen-minute period. Our log indicated that we triaged and treated more than 2,500 casualties during the siege.

The dramatic story of that epic battle has been told in literally thousands of books, newspaper articles, personal recollections, and even TV documentaries (e.g., on PBS), and although Charlie Med is mentioned in many of these reports, the real story of the four physicians and twenty-six corpsmen who provided surgical care for these men has never really been told. In telling it now, I can only hope that it will provide some measure of recognition for a group of medical warriors who stood tall in the face of intense enemy fire and who provided life-saving care for badly wounded Marines.

It is a great sadness for me that I cannot recall the names of the individual corpsmen who served with us during this difficult time, but this part of my story is for them and for all of the Marines who fought for us on that tiny piece of red clay.

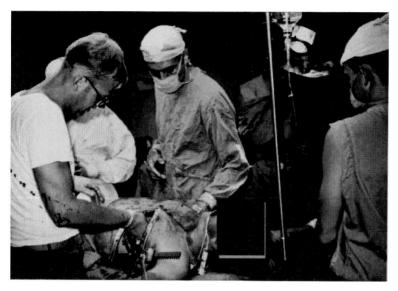

The author performs emergency open chest surgery to massage the heart

The author in an operating room at the combat base.

Birdseye view of the Khe Sanh Combat Base and Airstrip.

Chapter Seventeen

Casualty Care at Khe Sanh

Ed Feldman, from Forest Hills, New York, Don Magilligan from Brooklyn, New York, Joe Wolfe from Memphis, Tennessee, and me, Jim Finnegan, from Philadelphia, Pennsylvania—four physicians from four different cities, four different medical schools, and four different internships who later would practice in four different specialties, all of us in our mid-twenties, found ourselves meeting for the first time in a sandbagged tent while stabilizing wounded U.S. Marines and listening to the nearby explosions from incoming artillery fire. I doubt if any four other physicians could describe a more memorable first meeting. I still clearly remember that day, that moment: the four of us in fatigues, helmets, and flak jackets with .45s strapped to our sides. The presence of casualties and the immediate arrival of more wounded limited our initial greetings to nods of "hello." Without discussion, each of us moved into position to assess a wound, begin treatment, and order appropriate disposition of the injured. The corpsmen, likewise, needed no prompting, but worked seamlessly with us to treat and stabilize these injured men. It was about two hours later that we had medevaced the last man out and the guys showed me to my new "home," an –eight-by-ten-foot bunker dug into the ground with a roof of wooden planks covered with several layers of sandbags. It would be home to the four of us for the next three months.

As always with physicians, the initial conversation centered around our respective training credentials. Don, Ed, and Joe had all completed one year of internship after medical school. I was in my third year of surgical residency at the Hospital of the University of Pennsylvania. We did not share it at the moment, but as our friendship developed and allowed for more open discussion, it turned out that for a variety of reasons, all of us had volunteered for duty in Vietnam.

My Khe Sanh education began immediately. You were never

to walk directly up the wooden catwalk that ran from our bunker past the corpsmen's bunker to the triage area. Snipers apparently had targeted that area and it was strongly suggested that you zigzag your way up. The holes in the tents were from shrapnel and it was frequently necessary to kneel or lie down while treating a casualty during heavy incoming artillery. Casualties out on the ground, waiting for medevac choppers, were covered with flak jackets if we were taking incoming fire while trying to get them out. All these rules became second nature instantaneously, inasmuch as they were all related to the basic concept of survival in a hostile environment.

It soon became difficult to distinguish one day from another. The wounded arrived at all hours, sometimes one or two at a time and at other times one or two dozen, totaling over twenty-five hundred during the three months of the siege. It may seem impossible to believe today, but we took care of each one of them in a timely and appropriate fashion. To this day, we repeatedly affirm and reaffirm that no wounded Marine ever received anything but the best possible treatment even under unrelenting incoming fire. I fear I may overuse the phrase "incoming fire," but it would be impossible to tell the true story of Charlie Med without emphasizing that much of the story unfolds while the base underwent almost constant bombardment by enemy gunners.

As the triage tent became progressively shredded by shrapnel, it was apparent that we could not continue to attend to the wounded in that environment. I went to a regimental briefing, as I did most mornings, and indicated to Col. David Lownd's executive officer that if he wanted to prevent his wounded men from being rewounded, we needed a stronger facility. A few days later, the Seabees showed up with a bulldozer and dug a twelve-by-twenty-foot hole, braced it with heavy wooden beams, and covered it with steel matting left over from the construction of the airstrip. We suddenly had an underground triage bunker that allowed us to stand in relative safety. They even constructed a ramp down into the bunker so that the litter bearers didn't have to worry about tripping on steps, especially when lugging one of the heavier grunts.

Charlie Med's basic function was stabilization, the classic ABCs of trauma care—airway, breathing, and circulation. Each of the litter wounded was stripped naked, as previously mentioned, and all rifles, and all ammunition and grenades, were thrown into the "ammo box." Although we thought nothing of it at the time, to this day I get the heebie-jeebies when I recall how casually we tossed around all that live ordnance.

One of the first lessons learned in the assessment of combat injuries is that you are usually dealing with extremely high velocity projectiles which can and do find their way into every nook, crevice, and cranny of the human body. We did examine every armpit, every anal and perianal area, palpated every scalp, and rolled everybody, looking for occult entry and/or exit wounds. This effort was redoubled when we encountered, as we so frequently did, a young man in overt hemorrhagic shock with no immediately visible explanation. We learned quickly that an exploding mine can send shrapnel fragments up through the rectum and genitalia into abdominal and vascular structures. Any casualty with severe lower extremity injuries always had a very careful examination of his lower torso. Shrapnel wounds of the axilla and posterior scalp were not at all uncommon and always needed to be thought of and searched for.

The airway was always the first priority and we did not hesitate to intubate anyone who appeared to be struggling to breathe. Remember, there was no way then to check pulse oximetry or to run a blood gas. As a matter of fact, there was no lab there at all. We received regular deliveries of blood via chopper and all of it was transfused on a type-specific basis. Interestingly, I don't recall ever seeing a transfusion reaction.

Starting a large-bore intravenous line on a cold, dirty, wounded Marine was never an easy task. We routinely did saphenous vein cutdowns in the groin where that vein is largest and inserted thick IV tubing directly into it, thus enabling us to rapidly infuse large volumes of blood and other necessary fluids. Many wounds could be temporarily controlled with pressure dressings. Many required ligation, or the tying off of bleeding vessels.

The insertion of large-bore chest tubes was also a common event. In spite of the availability and use of flak jackets with their protective Kevlar panels, some Marines, especially on warmer days, chose to leave the fronts of their jackets open and were thus more susceptible to penetrating chest injuries.

The most dramatic cases were the young Marines who arrived with wounds so egregious that they had lost most of their blood volume and were in profound shock. The maximum team effort was required to salvage these badly wounded boys. Endotracheal intubation (insertion of a breathing tube), open cardiac massage, and the rapid infusion of large amounts of blood and other fluids were accomplished smoothly by my team of doctors and corpsmen. Those who did not survive were really dead on arrival, but we never hesitated to put on the full-court press, simply because we all knew that a previously healthy nineteen-year-old Marine could possess reserves that you can never underestimate. The truly amazing thing is that we were able to stabilize so many of them and medevac them to a more sophisticated facility.

When one thinks back to forty years ago, one may legitimately question my ability to reconstruct the events that occurred at that time with any degree of accuracy or reliability. There are two reasons why I think it is possible to do so. First, the siege of Khe Sanh was perhaps the preeminent story of the war in Vietnam and was widely covered by the world. I have been gifted with three large cocktail-table books on Vietnam and Khe Sanh as well as many novels that are devoted partially or entirely to this famous battle.

Secondly, I have been privileged for forty years to have Ed Feldman as my friend, confidant, and all-around source of the good life and great information. Eddie was such an important part of our surgical team at Charlie Med and was there for the entire siege. Many of the twenty-five hundred casualties owe their lives and good health to his skills as a physician and his incredible steadfastness under fire. He has received a Silver Star for an unbelievable act of gallantry and has been nominated for the

Medal of Honor. His story could easily be the subject of another book. On top of all of that, he has the most incredible memory of our time at Khe Sanh and can instantly recall people and events in great detail. He kept a diary the entire time and has shared it with me. In many ways, he is the co-author of this story.

We fought hard to save these boys. In retrospect, one of the great sadnesses of the whole experience is that we rarely knew their names. There was really very little time to develop the famous doctor-patient relationship. When I do recall specific cases, it is almost invariably in terms of the actual wound, the impact it had on the surgeon or surgical team, and what was done to the patient; and yes, I do think of them as patients. We never meant any disrespect toward any casualty and certainly did not intend to depersonalize the care we were rendering, but the sheer volume of the wounded necessitated a somewhat clipped approach, and we would refer to an injured man by the injured part: for example, "Don, check that belly on station 3," "Ed, are we going to have to intubate the chest wound?" The vast majority of the wounded were usually addressed as "Marine," as in "Take it easy, Marine, you're going to be okay."

I have referred to my time at Khe Sanh as a watershed moment in my life. Eddie has the same feeling. No, we didn't get religion or lose it. We didn't alter our career plans. I believe our values and personalities remained the same. What really changed was our sense of ourselves. Although most of the world didn't notice or perhaps didn't even care, we felt a tremendous sense of accomplishment having triaged, treated, operated upon, or stabilized and medevaced over twenty-five hundred wounded Marines. And we did it while under some of the most intense incoming artillery, mortar, and rocket fire ever recorded in such a small area.

We were just a couple of doctors in the earliest phase of our professional lives who found themselves in this remarkable arena and we did okay. We ducked but did not flinch. We treated each Marine like he was priority one. We protected them, sometimes with our own bodies, until they were out of harm's way. Not every day ended perfectly, of course. People we worked closely with were shot, sometimes fatally, but we knew the joys of saving a man and the gut-wrenching feeling of losing one. We tacitly understood the need to keep working even when it was extremely dangerous to do so. We did the job we came to do.

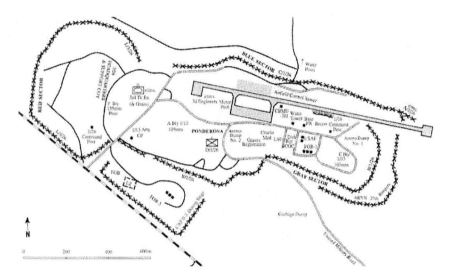

The Khe Sanh Combat Base - Charlie Med is located near the center of the base, immediately adjacent to the airstrip. The entire base was approximately 1 mile by 1/2 mile in size.

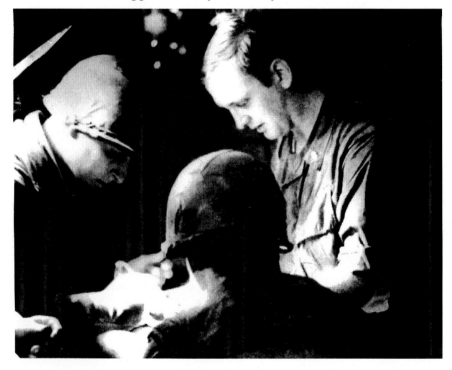

Drs. Feldman and Finnegan working on a casualty in the triage bunker at Khe Sanh

Charlie Med's surgical team during the siege. All were
Navy doctors who volunteered for Vietnam and were
assigned to the Third Marine Division. From left: Joe
Wolfe, Jim Finnegan, Ed Feldman and Don Magilligan.

Chapter Eighteen

They Were Heroes Once and Young

At times, the flow of casualties seemed almost never-ending. This flow of wounded men through Charlie Med depended heavily upon our ability to call in helicopters to fly them in when wounded and out after we had treated their wounds and stabilized their vital signs.

I believe that every chopper pilot and their crew, who flew in and out of Khe Sanh, frequently under heavy fire and at enormous risk, should have automatically received serious consideration for high-level decorations. These were amongst the bravest men I have ever seen in action. Their designation of their helicopters as "mortar magnets" was well deserved.

As the Khe Sanh combat base sat on an open plateau, it is easy to understand that enemy observers had a very clear view of approaching choppers. The base was only one mile long by a half mile wide in total size and was nearly completely surrounded by enemy positions. Charlie Med, of course, sat immediately adjacent to the airstrip. As a helicopter approached, our guys would crouch against nearby sandbags with their stretchers ready. We knew that the chopper wanted to spend an absolute minimum time on the ground so as soon as it touched down, our guys would rush to its door, lift the wounded onto the stretchers, and race to the triage bunker. If the chopper had battle orders, it left empty, meaning without patients, but if not, it would sit for an additional risky minute or two while we onloaded treated casualties who were stable enough to be medevaced.

Something that was very vital to our unit was being able to resupply it. We had an almost constant need for blood, splints, dressings, and instruments. Chest tubes, endotracheal tubes, and suture materials were used in significant quantities and at times very rapidly. During the early weeks of the siege, fixed-wing aircraft were still permitted to fly in and out of Khe Sanh. They would bring us larger quantities of material and could fly out more men but they were slow and cumbersome, making themselves inviting targets for NVA gunners. Let it be known that the end of Khe Sanh's runway was called the "Graveyard" because it was so close to enemy lines. Unfortunately, not every aircraft that taxied down that runway made it out.

As the fighting escalated, only choppers were permitted to fly into the combat base. They became our lifeline. We had a nearly constant need for supplies, and the choppers never let us down. Sometimes weather conditions were so adverse that all missions to Khe Sanh were on a purely volunteer basis. Those guys came nonetheless, with little regard for their own personal safety. The rotors kept rotating, the pilot and copilot sat resolutely at the controls, the door gunners helped to offload men or supplies and, if necessary, take on new medevacs.

One of my biggest regrets is that I never had a chance to meet with or to speak to any of the men who flew those missions.

I can only hope that some of them will read this and know that the surgical team of Charlie Med, Khe Sanh, regards them as great, if unrecognized, heroes to whom we owe an unpayable debt.

Chapter Nineteen

Spicer

The story of Jonathan Spicer was front-page news in early 1968. From the time of his first contact with the Marines, he tried to explain to them that he would do whatever was asked of him except to shoot a gun at anyone. Apparently, no one listened because before he knew it, he was on a hill outside of the Khe Sanh Combat Base with the Twenty-sixth Marine Regiment. Much to the dismay of his superiors, he continued to indicate that he would not shoot at anyone. To the Marines' credit, instead of punishing him, they sent him to me at Charlie Med where we put him to work as a litter bearer. It was extremely hazardous work.

During the siege, the base received, at times, over two thousand rounds of incoming mortar, rocket, and artillery fire per day. This was not random fire.

The NVA had forward observers who pinpointed targets for their gunners and one of their very favorite targets was a helicopter landing in front of Charlie Med to drop off newly wounded casualties or pick up those we had treated. The choppers were labeled "mortar magnets" because whenever one landed, it invariably drew fairly intense enemy fire. It was precisely at those times that we had to run to the helopad and offload the newly wounded or onload the treated Marines for evacuation to Dong Ha.

The chopper pilots sat calmly at their controls, rotors whirring and shells exploding, but never lifted off until we had safely moved every Marine. The Navy doctors and corpsmen, with Spicer as one of them, went back and forth from the helicopter to the triage bunker, carrying the wounded on canvas litters. I still don't understand why more of us weren't killed or wounded. Unfortunately, Spicer was not so lucky.

One day while most of us were in the bunker treating

the latest batch of the wounded, I heard someone yell, "Spicer's down." Seconds later two corpsmen arrived with Spicer on a litter. He appeared pale and lifeless. Ed Feldman, Joe Wolfe, Don Magilligan, and I moved as a team to his side. Dr. Joe Wolfe, a good ol' boy who had training in anesthesiology, quickly inserted a breathing tube. Dr. Eddie Feldman, who would go on to become a highly decorated physician war hero in his own right, began assessing Spicer for the location of any wound that might explain the absence of a pulse and blood pressure. Dr. Don Magilligan, who would later become one of America's leading heart surgeons, noticed Spicer's bulging neck veins and suggested that we might be dealing with cardiac tamponade, a condition in which blood builds up in the pericardium (heart sac), compresses the heart, and prevents it from pumping effectively. In a combat zone, that always means that a piece of shrapnel has hit the heart and made a small hole, which allows the blood to leak out and compress the heart.

I immediately opened the left side of his chest, opened the heart sac, and found a small hole in his left ventricle. With Don and Ed helping, I was able to place sutures (stitches) and close the hole. His heart began beating normally almost immediately and we all began smiling, yelling, and congratulating one another. It was, indeed, a joyous moment. We called for a medevac chopper, wrapped Spicer in bandages, and shipped him to the larger medical facility at the Dong Ha combat base.

After things calmed down, we heard the story of what happened. It seems that Spicer was carrying one end of a litter, taking a Marine to us for treatment. The man was fairly badly wounded and Spicer wanted to get him to us as fast as possible. When the incoming fire intensified, instead of ducking behind a row of sandbags lining the pathway from the helicopter to our bunker, he chose to keep moving and was hit in the chest with shrapnel.

Impressed? You should be. But you should also know that this was not his only act of heroism. Many times, as he was helping to move casualties and the incoming fire would intensify, he would put the litter on the ground, bend over the Marine, and shield him with his own body.

For many years I didn't know what happened to Jonathan Spicer. One of the frustrations of combat surgery is that the men pass through so quickly and there is no established mechanism for obtaining follow-up. Eventually, I learned that he was evacuated through the system to a military hospital in Japan where he died of "infection."

When I made my first visit to the Vietnam Wall, I traced his name onto a thin piece of paper. I still have it. Corporal Spicer was awarded the Navy Cross, the nation's second-highest military honor. I was glad to learn of that award, but somehow it doesn't seem enough for this gallant young man.

Chapter Twenty

Hair Today, Gone Tomorrow

During the siege, I was the commanding officer of a Navy surgical team comprised of four physicians and twenty-six corpsmen, all who cared for the casualties during the difficulty. We saw and treated nearly every conceivable kind of wound involving every part of the human body. The nature of some of these combat injuries and the surgical treatment of them have been well described elsewhere. Less well known and certainly less frequently discussed are the responses to combat and living under intense enemy fire that do not result in a wound and for which there are no medals.

One of our twenty-six corpsmen was Hospital Corpsman, Second Class Dan McMurtry. Besides being extremely handsome and sporting a full head of curly blond hair, he was one of our best, competent in every aspect of combat surgery and absolutely steadfast under fire. Whenever Charlie Med was receiving casualties and heavy incoming fire at the same time, I could always count on Dan to stay by my side and help me to do whatever was needed to stabilize a wounded Marine.

One day, halfway through the siege (at that time we had no idea when, if, or how this nightmare would end) Dan came to my bunker and asked to speak with me privately. We went outside and sat down behind a wall of sandbags. He quietly asked if I would medevac him to the rear. I immediately asked if he was hurt or wounded. He then answered by removing his helmet. He was completely and totally bald. The full head of thick, curly blond hair was gone. He was as bald as an eagle. I had no clue as to cause and immediately issued a medevac tag for him. He was back in Khe Sanh within two days with a note from a dermatologist in Da Nang diagnosing stress alopecia, a sudden loss of hair due to the enormous stress he was under. No treatment was available and none was recommended.

The diagnosis did not allow him to leave the war zone and he was therefore sent directly back to us to resume his duties as a corpsman. He never complained or questioned the decision. I'm very happy to report that by the time the siege had ended several weeks later, he had regrown some "peach fuzz."

Chapter Twenty-One

Arc Light

O n a tiny, red clay plateau in the northwest corner of South Vietnam, elements of the Third Marine Division built the Khe Sanh combat base, named after a nearby village occupied mostly by farmers. The base was about one mile long and a half a mile wide. The majority of the small space was covered by an airstrip made of steel Marston matting, built by the Seabees. Charlie Med was located immediately adjacent to the airstrip at its midpoint. For seventy-seven days during January, February, and March of 1968, that now-famous outpost was under siege by an estimated forty thousand North Vietnamese Army regulars. The base was defended by forty-eight hundred Marines. There was grave concern that General Giap, the commander of the North Vietnamese forces, intended to overrun the base just as he had at Dien Bien Phu when the French tried to hold onto that outpost.

President Lyndon B. Johnson followed the events at Khe Sanh on an hourly basis and was extremely concerned that the loss of Khe Sanh would represent a great military and moral victory for Giap, Ho Chi Minh, and the communist north. He actually had a sand model of the base constructed in the Situation Room of the White House. The media's exhaustive coverage of the siege on an almost hour-by-hour basis only served to heighten President Johnson's concern. He ordered his generals to use all possible means to save the base from destruction and had them sign a document pledging to carry out his order. Those of us on the base had no knowledge of the president's concern. All we knew for certain was that we were being pounded mercilessly.

The action in the air around us was never ending. Helicopters by the dozens would bring in supplies, fly casualties to us at Charlie Med, and then medevac them out after we had stabilized them. CH-46 Sea Knights with their double rotors and hydraulic rear gates and Huey gunships were regularly on our helopad just adjacent to the airstrip and routinely drew heavy enemy fire when they approached.

Fighter jets constantly screeched overhead, unleashing their fearsome weaponry on the enemy who were so close by. Their firepower was awesome and I was very thankful that the North Vietnamese did not have any airpower to add to the pounding we were already experiencing. But none of the air war compared to the B-52 bombing of Khe Sanh's perimeter. I can only surmise that the generals took the president very seriously when he ordered them to use all possible means to prevent the fall of Khe Sanh.

The code name for these air strikes was Arc Light. These huge B-52 Stratofortresses could carry a large number of five-hundred-pound bombs. When an entire bomber squadron dropped those monsters simultaneously, very little beneath them would be recognizable, let alone survive. Information obtained after the war indicated that the Vietnamese feared the B-52s more than anything else we had to offer in the way of firepower.

We were instructed that upon hearing the code Arc Light, we were to leave our bunkers and lay on the ground. Since we were under so much fire, so frequently, no one relished leaving his bunker, and the passing of the code words was usually greeted by a chorus of choice "combat" remarks such as "Why don't you stick the bombs up your ass?" or "Shit, another arc fucking light!"

But the advice to leave our bunkers during the Arc Light strikes proved sound, as several of the smaller bunkers did collapse due to the tremendous ground tremors produced when these mega, five-hundred-pound bombs exploded on the perimeter of this very small base with such deadly accuracy.

Chapter Twenty-Two

The Parachute Story

Fast-forward to March 1968. The siege of Khe Sanh is ongoing. NVA incoming is at record levels. The regimental briefings each morning, which I attended as commanding officer of Charlie Med, referred regularly and very seriously to the impending attempt by the NVA to overrun the base. I noted, with some concern, that one of the suggested attack routes, as determined by Marine intelligence, was right through Charlie Med. Inasmuch as we could see enemy troops about two hundred yards from the base perimeter, which was situated about twenty yards behind our facility, I waited until after the briefing and approached the regimental executive officer. I expressed my concern that if the attack did indeed come through Charlie Med, there was only one squad of Marines between them and us. We would, in all likelihood, be dealing with casualties and therefore not be in a very good position to protect ourselves, much less offer significant resistance. The major allowed as to how a reaction force would *immediately* be dispatched to our area to encounter the NVA onslaught. I then asked how long it would take for them (the reaction force) to get there. He said it would be twenty to thirty minutes at a minimum and could be longer if the NVA attacked in more than one area. I suggested to him that as physicians and corpsmen, we were probably not the world's greatest fighting machine. I reminded him that our only weapons were .45 pistols, which most of us carried unloaded for fear of blowing off one of our own feet. He asked me if we still had the policy of removing all weapons and ordnance from the wounded. I assured him that we did. To this day, I recall, with smirking astonishment, how we routinely took M16s, ammo clips, knives, and grenades off the wounded and casually threw them into the ammo box, from which they were retrieved by the Marines. The major suggested that the physicians and corpsmen of Charlie Med arm themselves with M16s, ammo clips, and grenades, dig fighting holes, and be prepared to defend the area until the promised reaction force arrived. I did indeed share this reassuring information with my men, but I also offered them my own alternate plan, which was, in the event that the NVA chose our unit to attack, we would all retreat to the adjacent airstrip and hide under the parachutes that had accumulated there after supplies were air-dropped onto the base. I was hoping that a little gallows humor might divert the crew's attention from the other, grimmer scenario. I don't think it worked. The reality of the situation, known to all of us, was that we were in deep shit.

Chapter Twenty-Three

My Close Encounters with the Fourth Estate

I observed a media incident that will forever be seared in my mind and will forever color my assessment of any reports I read. During the siege of Khe Sanh, there were many medical representatives on the base. I suppose one at least should give them credit for working under such hazardous conditions, but the accuracy of some of the reporting is a question in my mind.

One day as I was returning to Charlie Med after a briefing at regimental headquarters, the base began once again taking heavy incoming artillery fire. I saw a few people jump into a nearby bunker and I jumped in right after them. We all sat hunched over and curled up until we saw that the barrage seemed to have lessened, at which time we ventured into more of an upright sitting position. It was then that I saw that I was sharing the bunker with two African-American Marines and an older gentleman holding a microphone with a large spongelike round top. He tilted the instrument toward the two grunts and asked, "How are they treating the black Marines in Khe Sanh?" In polite company, I cannot tell you what I wanted to do with that microphone. To the everlasting credit of the two Marines, they gave him what one might call a dirty look and exited the bunker. Ah yes, objective reporting at its finest.

At the risk of being accused of media bashing, I will tell you one more story that continues to color my thinking about our colleagues in the fourth estate. The siege of Khe Sanh, as mentioned, received a great deal of media coverage. In fairness, it was one of the signature events of American involvement and was dramatically spotlighted by President Lyndon B. Johnson himself. Many of the events were widely publicized in the American press. I was featured in a few of those stories, and so my family knew I was there, and they were always concerned for my safety.

After the siege was over, I returned to the Dong Ha combat base. In correspondence with my family, I assured them that I was well and that it was highly unlikely that I would ever be in such danger as at Khe Sanh again. A few weeks later, I received a letter from home castigating me for breaking my promise. Enclosed was an article from the wire service published in the *Philadelphia Inquirer* with a headline that read, "Battle of Dong Ha Rages." Obviously, as a surgeon at Dong Ha, if the battle was raging, I would be acutely aware of it, as we would be receiving the wounded from such an encounter.

No battle of any sort had taken place. I happened to know the writer of the article and he was still in the area. I let it be known that I was looking for him and a few days later he showed up wondering what I wanted. I showed him the article and told him that it had frightened my family. I also pointed out that this battle had never occurred. He then proceeded to explain his way out of things. A recon patrol had found themselves pinned down and had called for reinforcements. A company of Marines arrived and the patrol was successfully rescued, incurring only light casualties. I was well aware of this action and told the reporter that that was in no way "The Battle of Dong Ha." He agreed with me immediately and explained that in order to maintain his position as a war correspondent he was required to submit war stories on a regular basis. At the time, the recon action was all that was available as fodder for an article, so he took it upon himself to indulge in a little creative writing. He promised not to do it again but didn't appear in the least apologetic.

Chapter Twenty-Four

It Ain't Easy Being Green

I don't believe anyone has ever told the story of Father "Chick" Kelly, a Navy chaplain stationed in Khe Sanh during the siege.

In March of 1968, he pulled off a feat that I believe is about as close to a miracle as I will ever get. In the late evening of March 17, just after dark, word was passed around that we should make our way to a certain bunker just down the road from Charlie Med. Ed, Don, and I did so to find Father Chick dishing out ice cream to everyone who entered the bunker. We had been living on C-rations for over two months, never having a taste of anything cold or creamy.

This was truly a monumental event for us and we went over to the good man for some dessert. We were incredulous to see that the ice cream was indeed green in honor of St. Patrick's Day.

Of course, we wanted to know how he had pulled off such a coup. He absolutely refused to disclose how it happened, not even under the pain of death. There was nothing that we could do or say to make him tell us how he obtained this green ice cream, which was delicious, by the way.

Father Kelly, unfortunately, would later sustain severe wounds, requiring his evacuation for urgent surgery followed by even more surgery and long months of painful rehabilitation, after which he would still walk with a limp.

Years later, I had the pleasure of reconnecting with Chick, who had long since left the priesthood and ultimately ended up in the real estate business. He still would not tell me how he got that green ice cream. To this day, he refuses to divulge his secret.

Chapter Twenty-Five

ADLs in Khe Sanh

" *T*ake *a shower." "Eat your breakfast." "Brush your teeth." "You're not going out in those dirty clothes." "Sit up straight in that chair." "Don't eat with your fingers—that's why God made utensils." "At least comb your hair."*

How many times did your mother resort to one of these old saws to at least attempt to keep you on the straight and narrow? In medical circles, the physical therapists and rehabilitation specialists refer to some of these things as "activities of daily living" or ADLs. After injury or serious illness, a patient's progress back to normal is frequently expressed in terms of their ability to accomplish some of these basic tasks.

At a recent reunion of the Third Medical Battalion in Charleston, South Carolina, some of the physicians were having a BS session over a few scotches when someone mentioned ADLs. A couple of the guys knew that I was trying to write about some of my Vietnam experiences and suggested that I write about our "activities of daily living" during the siege of Khe Sanh. Someone remarked that just living daily was an activity unto itself, but I thought it would be interesting to recall just how one did eat one's breakfast, or brush one's teeth, while the NVA tried to blast us off the face of the earth.

Having a bowel movement takes on a whole new meaning when you have to time it between mortar attacks. Try to imagine sitting on a piece of plywood with a hole cut in it that just barely accommodates one butt while wearing a steel helmet and flak jacket, with your pants down only just enough and your .45 resting on your thigh. I was equally afraid of incoming artillery and the possibility that I might shoot myself in the foot with my own gun. Suffice it to say, no one ever took reading material with them.

Over the years since Khe Sanh, Eddie Feldman and I have had the occasion to take our wives to fairly swanky hotels and resorts. He will usually ask me if the ultra luxurious bathroom in my suite reminds me of the facilities at Khe Sanh. I always respond that I seem to have been the beneficiary of a slight upgrade. In truth, we did not shower for nearly three months. I realize that sounds utterly incredible, but it is the truth. First off, I don't think a shower even existed, or at least I was unaware of one.

Secondly, while you might be willing to risk life and limb for a two-minute bowel movement while armed and wearing a helmet and flak jacket, no one in his right mind was going to risk standing naked, protected only by clouds and sunshine, just to wash off a little blood and red dirt. When everyone smells the same, it becomes less of a problem.

The absence of a laundry facility did not in any way affect the casualties, because we used disposable materials. For the doctors, corpsmen, and Marines, however, the concept of clean clothing was a distant memory. When you're being dropped into a hot fire zone by a fast-moving chopper, you don't want to be slowed down by carrying a three-month supply of skivvies.

Besides, I never imagined I'd be there that long, a thought shared by many new arrivals to Khe Sanh. I don't remember when we simply stopped wearing underwear, but I do recall going a long time without any. The problem was that our jungle fatigues became encrusted with blood and mud and were capable of standing on their own without a human inside. Rumor aside, we did not clean our bayonets on our pant legs.

I wonder if Mom would have encouraged us to clean our plates if the meal consisted of C-rations. These boxed and canned food items were standard issue for all combat troops from World War II through the Vietnam conflict. A can of fruit cocktail was a cherished find, while ham and lima beans was perhaps the most disliked dish of all time. One of the favorite pastimes of military personnel was giving creative nicknames to food items available to the troops. Most of them could not be repeated in Mom's kitchen. During my time on active duty, I never heard anyone ask for creamed chip beef on toast. Everyone called it SOS—"shit on a shingle." There is no other nickname for any food item that struck me and stuck with me as much as the grunt's designation for ham and lima beans, that all too common component of C-rations in Vietnam. This tasty dish was referred to as ham and motherfuckers, a rather profane title but one that will live on forever in unauthorized military dictionaries. The ease with which that phrase slides off of one's tongue continues to amaze me.

Years later, Ed Feldman and I were having dinner with our wives, Linda and Patty. The girls were, as usual, talking about kids, clothes, weddings, and so on, while Ed and I were leaning into each other having one of our sotto voce talks about sex, war, love, and food, not necessarily in that order. The waiter stopped to see if we had made our menu choices and almost spontaneously, Ed whispered to me that we should inquire as to whether they were serving ham and motherfuckers. Unfortunately, the ladies overheard the remarks. We laughingly apologized and explained the C-ration lingo to them. I thought the matter was closed and forgotten until several months later I came home from work and inquired as to what was for dinner. Without hesitating or looking away from the stove, my very proper, Emily Post–quoting wife said, "Ham and motherfuckers."

Chapter Twenty-Six

The Awards Ceremony

In late June of 1968 the Third Marine Division had moved its headquarters from Dong Ha to Quang Tri. I had now been "in country" nearly ten months and was very close to becoming a "short timer," which is anyone with less than thirty days to go in a twelve-month tour. A couple of new surgeons had arrived, so my workload was lighter than it had been all year.

A notice came out of Third Marine Division headquarters that an awards ceremony was to be held at Quang Tri and our medical battalion commanding officer, Bob Brown, instructed Ed Feldman and me to attend. I had no idea why, and if Ed knew, he wasn't saying.

On the appointed day we choppered down and joined a

group of ten or eleven other guys in the middle of the "parade ground," which was really a little dirt field where we used to play volleyball. I asked Eddie what the hell was going on, but he just smiled and said that I should just shut the fuck up and pay fucking attention.

Moments later, someone shouted "Attention," we stiffened, and Maj. Gen. Raymond Davis, one of the most highly decorated Marines of all time, and a two-star Marine general appeared, accompanied by a small entourage of other lower-ranking officers, one of whom was carrying some sort of a pillow covered with medals.

Ed Feldman was standing to my immediate left. The general pinned a very pretty medal on his chest, which I was soon to learn was a Silver Star being awarded to him for removing a live mortar round from a Marine's abdomen. As is typical for Ed, he never uttered a word about his incredible heroism to me or anyone else. Later we would tease him that the medal was actually for getting laid on R&R more than anyone else in the Third Marine Division

As the general approached me, I was still seriously wondering just what in the hell I was doing there. Then he pinned a Purple Heart on my chest. He remarked that he had not had many opportunities to pin a Purple Heart on a physician and asked where I was wounded. I was tempted to reply, "In the ass and the arm," which was the truth, but politely responded that I had sustained minor shrapnel wounds from an incoming mortar round during the siege of Khe Sanh but didn't report it and didn't think anyone noticed. He shook my hand a second time, while gripping my forearm with his left hand. "Thank you," he said, and I swear he was misty eyed as he moved on to the next man. Turns out that Eddie and our corpsmen had entered my name into the casualty log without telling me. I was, of course, extremely proud but also a little embarrassed. My wounds were small and, compared to the egregious wounds I had been treating for the past ten months, really quite insignificant. As usual, Ed set me straight with a cryptic, "It could have been in your fucking eye."

The awards ceremony at the Quang Tri Base

Ed Feldman with his Silver Star and me with my Purple Heart

Chapter Twenty-Seven

Eddie Feldman

You've seen it dozens of times: an unexploded shell or bomb is located in a precarious position and unless it is removed or defused, the entire city or world will be blown to smithereens. Invariably, one heroic individual steps up and attempts the nerve-wracking task of defusing the explosive at his or her own personal risk. On TV and in the movies, given a fair amount of sweat and shakes, the hero is successful, usually seconds before Armageddon occurs. It's good stuff. It keeps you on the edge of the chair with an increased pulse and sweaty palms. We all imagine that we, too, would function like that in those situations just like the hero did; but would we?

I know someone who did just that—Ed Feldman, Dr. Ed Feldman, Lieutenant Ed Feldman, my friend Eddie—the greatest war hero I have personally ever known. Who in the hell is Eddie Feldman? If he's so much a hero, why didn't they retire his uniform and hang it alongside Sgt. York's or Audie Murphy's? Well, I'll tell you what, if he did what he did during World War II or the Korean War, which enjoyed the backing of every red- and blue-blooded American, he'd probably have a statue in Washington, DC, or at least a very large plaque in Los Angeles. As it was, his heroism occurred in Vietnam while the antiwar movement was nearing its peak in the United States and all but drowning out or flatly rejecting any possibility of good news from Southeast Asia. The Marines noticed what he did. I noticed too, but the rest of the world did not notice and could have cared less.

What exactly did Lieutenant Feldman do? In military terms, he received the Silver Star for gallantry. The citation accompanying that medal mentions such things like "uncommon valor" and "total disregard for personal danger," but no citation can adequately describe the scene that unfolded that day in Vietnam.

Dr. Feldman was out in the field with a company of Marines who were taking heavy incoming fire. One of the casualties scared the living bejeezus out of everyone when they realized that an unexploded shell was embedded in his abdominal wall near his liver. No one wanted to touch the guy, let alone move him. Eddie calmly came on the scene, ordered everyone out of the way, reassured the frightened Marine (who was awake), and then slowly removed the shell from the poor Marine's abdomen. The shell was then taken from the area and detonated. The Marine lived; Ed Feldman was decorated with a Silver Star and became a true grunt hero known but to a few.

I suppose it would be easy to write this off as one more amazing-but-true war story, but think about it for a moment. Same scene except you're in Lieutenant Feldman's position. Conjure up the picture in your mind. Contemplate how much of you would be found if that mortar round exploded. Ignore the possibility of moving the Marine, evacuating him, or passing on the risk to others. Step up, take hold of the shell in your bare hands, bare face, bare everything. Lift it out of the grunt's belly and then have it safely moved out of harm's way. After that, simply dress the wound and go about your business. How about a million bucks and the Congressional Medal of Honor?

There is more. There actually was no such thing as "business as usual" for Lieutenant Feldman. He could have and should have stayed at the Delta Med section of the Dong Ha combat base and helped to care for casualties in a safely bunkered triage area but not Eddie.

Every time a Marine platoon or company got involved in a firefight, took casualties, and screamed for a doctor, Eddie would grab his M16 and jump on a helicopter to fly out into the midst of the action and administer to the Marine casualties. You should know that there are trauma experts who think that physicians can do little under such circumstances and that the most expeditious way of caring for such combat casualties is to quickly load them onto helicopters and get them back to a combat base where surgical teams can take care of them. Tell it to the Marines. If you're not already a rabid fan of Eddie's, let me share with you another aspect of his personality and performance.

There is one more thing I have to tell you about Dr. Ed Feldman. He has been nominated for the Medal of Honor for yet another incredible performance. Because the matter has not yet been fully adjudicated, I'll keep this short. In September of

1967, a company of U.S. Army soldiers was pinned down and in danger of being overrun by a large enemy force. Ed jumped on a chopper and was flown into the battle scene, where he not only administered to the casualties, but helped direct some of the fighting because the Army officers in the unit had already been killed or wounded. Two army sergeants who were there wrote descriptions of Ed's actions, and their eyewitness reports are the basis for the Medal of Honor nomination. I have no idea what the military bureaucracy will do with this petition, but if anyone's individual and collective acts of true heroism ever deserved such recognition, that man is Ed Feldman.

Somehow, a Silver Star seems inadequate. I don't know much about the military, and certainly not much about their criteria for issuing combat decorations. It seems that most of them are for singular acts of heroism, but how do you reward dozens or even hundreds of acts of heroism like the ones that Eddie carried out—deeds most men won't even contemplate, let alone perform? The answer, of course, is that there is no adequate reward or recognition.

I have been privileged to have Eddie as a dear and much-loved friend for forty years. I can only hope that others who read this will come to admire him as I do.

Chapter Twenty-Eight

Purple Heart

I've never talked about it before but I promised myself that if I ever developed enough self-discipline and stick-to-itiveness to actually write the story of Charlie Med at Khe Sanh, I would tell the story of how I received my Purple Heart.

It happened on February 29, 1967, so I guess I only get to celebrate once every four years. We were in our bunker when the sound of approaching choppers told us of the arrival of new casualties. Four of us began to zigzag up the catwalk to the triage bunker when, as usual, the ever-vigilant NVA gunners began lobbing shells onto the base, targeting the newly arrived helicopter. I was about ten feet from the bunker door when a mortar round exploded very close to me. I remember the force of the blast just as much as I remember feeling what seemed like a few hundred little stinging sensations. The shell must have landed just behind me because the violent air movement literally blew me down the steps into the triage bunker. I remember moving my feet and legs as fast as I could to prevent myself from falling down the steps. I was certain that the round went off directly under me, but my buddies assured me that had that been the case, it would be highly unlikely that I would have been standing there talking to them.

When the dust settled, it turned out that I had a small shrapnel wound on my left forearm which did not require serious care. The remainder of the stings remained undefined. As we did not often undress or change clothes, I never knew at the time whether the stings represented tiny pieces of shrapnel or just dirt and rocks propelled by the force of the explosion. I later learned that they were called "salt-and-pepper wounds."

Unbeknownst to me, someone entered my name in the casualty log and several months later I was surprised to be called to a ceremony where Major General Raymond Davis pinned the

Purple Heart on my uniform.Believe me, I am so, so proud of it but at the same time, I can't help feeling that I really shouldn't have the same medal as the very seriously wounded Marines that we were caring for.

I have been tempted to write to the higher military authorities and ask if they had a smaller size.

Chapter Twenty-Nine

Truly Great Men

Throughout this book, I have told you stories of men whom I considered to be real heroes. Lt. Bill Gay, First Platoon, A Company of the Third Engineer Battalion, risked his own life during the siege of Khe Sanh to save a visiting reporter. He could have simply dove for cover and saved himself, but he shielded her body with his own and pushed her into a bunker. During those few seconds an artillery round exploded next to him, resulting in multiple major injuries that required many operations and years of rehabilitation to correct. He did finally accept a Purple Heart, having not even reported the previous two times he was wounded. He received no other medal for his actions.

You would stand up and salute him if you knew the total true story of Ed Feldman's heroism. He was awarded a Silver Star for removing a live mortar round from the abdomen of a young marine. But Lt. Edward Feldman, Medical Corps U.S. Navy, assigned to the Third Marine Division, Vietnam, performed above and beyond the call of duty on many other occasions, frequently under heavy enemy fire, most of which were never recorded or rewarded.

I could tell you so many stories about Marines and Navy corpsmen and helicopter pilots whose bravery and courage, in the face of conditions that no one should ever have to face, were known only to the men around them. If my wartime experience taught me anything, it is that for every Sergeant York and Audie Murphy, there are hundreds if not thousands of unsung heroes whose songs will never be sung. There are, of course, parallels in the civilian world. I have witnessed examples of courage and selfless behavior and have thought intuitively that these individuals would perform very well, perhaps extraordinarily well, in adverse tactical situations.

I have one man particularly in mind. Even though he was a lifelong practicing Quaker, his name comes always to mind when someone asks, "Who would you like to have next to you in a foxhole?" I suspect he would roll over in his grave if he heard me discuss him in this context, but my professor of surgery at the Hospital of the University of Pennsylvania, Jonathan E. Rhoads, MD, was a man of such mental and moral strength, a man who valued human life so much that he dedicated his entire surgical career to improving it. I have no doubt that his performance in the face of hostile fire would have identified him as a true hero. But he remained true to the Quaker tradition and was a true pacifist. When I went to him in mid-1967 and told him that I felt that I had to volunteer for duty in Vietnam, a war to which he was naturally strongly opposed, he never mentioned his own feelings. Instead, he first informed me that it was a long-established tradition in the Department of Surgery at Penn that if a man left to serve his country, his place in the program would be saved until he returned. He then took out a piece of paper, wrote for a moment, and handed it to me. It contained his name and a phone number. "That's my home phone number. Give it to your family and tell them to call me if they need anything while you are gone." I will never forget that moment. As the years went by, I learned more and more about this great man. His integrity, intellectual honesty, and incredible personal strength of character are characteristics that many aspire to but few achieve. This much I know for certain—if, at any time, Dr. Rhoads chose to take sides in a fight—civilian, military, or otherwise—you would want to be very certain you were on his side.

Chapter Thirty

A Kiss Is Just a Kiss or R&R—Part I

In July 1968, while I was in Dong Ha, Bob Brown, the commanding officer of the Third Medical Battalion, called me into his hooch and told me that, as a reward for my service in Khe Sanh during the siege, he was giving me an R&R to Bangkok, Thailand. In truth, I had no great interest in going to Bangkok, but decided that it had to be a damned sight better than sitting where I was. I had to go to Da Nang on July 11 to catch my flight to Bangkok. As it turned out, I arrived in Da Nang one day early as the actual plane to Thailand was not leaving until the 12th. Not wishing to sleep once again under the tail of a fighter jet, I asked a young Marine lieutenant for directions to the "White Elephant," the pseudonym for the officers' club nearest the airport. He not only knew where it was, but offered to take me there in his jeep. What followed was one of the most unusual experiences of my entire life.

It was about 8 o'clock when I walked into the officers' club and took a seat at the bar. I had barely sipped my first scotch when a USO show, consisting of a trio of beautiful, sexy, and vocally talented Philippine women, began. It was the best (only?) entertainment I had seen in the Republic of Vietnam. They were terrific, and when I discovered that there would be several more performances, I decided to stay there longer. I struck up a conversation with the guy sitting next to me, who was a Marine captain. He asked where I had been and when I told him that I was the CO of the surgical team in Khe Sanh during the siege, he shook my hand and said that I was his guest for the remainder of my time at the club that evening. Toward midnight, after more USO entertainment, and even more drinks, I explained to the good captain that I had to leave as I had a plane to catch for my R&R in Bangkok, indicating in the same breath that it was not my first choice. He laughed and said, "Who the hell do you think you've been drinking with all evening?" He then went on to explain that after being wounded three times, he was taken out of combat and made the commanding officer of the R&R center. He told me to forget Thailand as he could send me to Australia, Hong Kong, or any R&R destination of my choice. I immediately chose Hong Kong. He said that was a great choice because the flight was not leaving until the day after tomorrow and he was taking me to an all-night party with some friends of his—the Special Forces. My enthusiasm for this adventure diminished considerably when we left the club and climbed into a vehicle with a .50-caliber machine gun mounted on the back manned by a young Marine. It turned out that the Special Forces friends of his occupied a villa on the outskirts of Da Nang and we would have to travel through some unsecured areas to get there. I'm sure it was the scotch that helped me to take this ride with some degree of equanimity.

We arrived at the villa by some miracle unscathed. It was a stately white French colonial mansion with flowered verandas. There was a beautiful cool breeze that evening with no discernible humidity. A number of young, attractive Vietnamese women were moving about quietly and remained quite unobtrusive throughout the night. Jack (not the Marine captain's real name) and I ended up sitting at a table on the veranda with a staff sergeant and first lieutenant from the Special Forces. Jack's record as a thrice-wounded combat company commander qualified him to sit with these Green Berets, who, I could see, considered themselves to be great warriors. I sensed they were a little uncertain as to why I had been allowed to come to their private place, but when Jack told them that I was wounded in Khe Sanh while treating wounded Marines, they welcomed me into their circle.

We enjoyed our drinks while Jack and the two Berets talked, with me just listening. At one point, the sergeant looked at me and said that while he very much appreciated my Khe Sanh experience, it probably did not allow me to know, feel, or understand the incredibly intense bond that develops between men who stand together in hand-to-hand combat with the enemy and survive together as blood brothers. Before I could respond, he and the Special Forces lieutenant turned towards each other, embraced tightly and then proceeded to open-mouth French kiss each other for several seconds. After disengaging, the sergeant turned to me and asked what I thought. When I replied that I thought they were both probably closet homosexuals, the sergeant came over the table at me, only to be intercepted by Jack who handled him easily and sat him back down.

Shortly thereafter, we were racing back to Da Nang in our jeep. I was still shaking a bit, but Jack thought the whole thing was hilarious. Anyway, as promised, the next day I flew out to Hong Kong.

Before I tell you about my experience when I finally reached Hong Kong, I have to describe the scene at the Da Nang "airport" as I boarded the flight. It is tradition or protocol in the military that boarding and disembarking an aircraft is done according to certain rules. It so happens that my flight was filled with 124 enlisted men, two Air Force nurses (officers), and me. As the senior officer, I was told, I would board last. The female officers were told to board first, followed by all the Marines. I was amazed upon entering the aircraft to see that all the Marines had completely bypassed the women, who were seated in front of the plane. Naturally, I felt it my duty to sit with the nurses, only to discover that the one next to me was a born-again Christian whose only interest was trying to get me to do some Bible readings with her. (I swear, Ed, that's all it was.)

Chapter Thirty-One

R&R–Part II

After landing, we were bused to the R&R center and lectured briefly about how to behave appropriately while visiting this famous international city. We were also told to select a hotel and, lacking any prior significant travel experience, I chose the Hong Kong Hilton, perhaps not the most exotic choice, but one that would lead me to a most unusual stay in a most unusual city.

The hotel check-in process took me through a remarkably beautiful lobby whose dramatic oriental motif, even today, remains clear in my mind. One of the many amenities was a gorgeous pool, and having lived in Vietnam for the past nine months under somewhat less than luxurious circumstances, I decided that a nice swim would be my first priority. I had a pair of gym shorts that served as my bathing suit and within moments of check-in, I was in the pool.

The first thing I noticed was that no one was speaking English, an unusual auditory phenomenon for a kid from Pittsburgh, Pennsylvania. I did the breaststroke slowly around the pool listening to some German conversation (I had taken two years of high school German so I knew what it was). Many people were speaking in various Asian dialects, none of which I could specifically identify. As I swam toward the far end of the pool, I thought I detected an English conversation. I kept moving in that direction and came upon a young couple facing each other while holding on to the side of the pool. I swam up to them, apologized for interrupting, and explained that they were the only English-speaking people I had been able to identify. They were extremely cordial and invited me to join them in conversation. We exchanged information and I explained that I was a Navy surgeon assigned to the U.S. Marine Corps in Vietnam. The gentleman insisted that I provide him with the details of my experiences over cocktails and dinner.

After the greatest shower I have ever taken in my life, I dressed and met my new friends, Mike and Carol, in the lobby. We went by taxi to a restaurant that I can still picture but whose name I cannot remember. While exiting the cab, I reached for my wallet so as to pay the driver, but Mike grabbed my hand and said that he would pay. He insisted that I was to be their guest for the next week and would not be permitted to spend any of my own money. I brushed him off lightly and said that dinner was on me. As we took our seats in the restaurant, I couldn't help but notice that while there were quite a few people lined up at the maitre d's podium, we were seated immediately with quite a bit of flourish and bowing. Cocktails arrived quickly and Mike asked if I would tell him and Carol more about myself and my time in Vietnam. He seemed genuinely interested, but it wasn't until later that I would understand why.

I told them briefly about my surgical training at the Hospital of the University of Pennsylvania, a little something about boot camp with the Marines at Camp Lejuene, North Carolina, and then rather superficially summarized my time in Vietnam, including a mention of the siege of Khe Sanh where I was the commanding officer of a surgical team.

They were very much aware of the extensive media coverage of the siege and fascinated by the fact that I had actually been there during that dramatic and much-publicized battle. I don't think I wanted very much to go into detail about my experience there and so I asked them to tell me about themselves.

Mike was thirty-three years old and had graduated from the University of Michigan at age twenty-two with a degree in economics. He didn't want to go immediately to graduate school and the job market for a young man with a BA in economics and no other credentials or experience was almost nonexistent. He decided to go to Oklahoma and find a job in the oil fields as a laborer. He signed on as a wildcatter with a small oil drilling company. He said he made a decent amount of money but had no outlet for spending it and after a few years had accumulated quite a tidy sum. He then learned of an opportunity to buy a few thousand dollar units of a company in the natural gas drilling business and decided, as young men will do, to go for it. The rest, as they say, is history. The company struck natural gas, his shares increased exponentially in value, and at the tender age of thirty he was a millionaire many times over. He met Carol before the strike and they had fallen in love. They then decided to tour the world and I met them on the Far Eastern leg of their journey. Carol was as beautiful and gracious as Mike was kind and generous.

On our final night together, they took me to the penthouse restaurant of the Mandarin Hotel. The exquisite oriental décor was very impressive and I'll never forget the overwhelming beauty of the room. We sat on plush pillows around low tables and were served an endless variety of excellent food, most of which Mike had to identify for me. The highlight of the evening was a fashion show. The models were incredibly beautiful Asian and Eurasian girls. Each time a model would pass by us Mike would look at Carol to see if she liked or wanted the outfit. Carol would discreetly shake her head, which relieved me greatly as the announced prices of some of the garments ranged from two to ten thousand dollars.

The finale was a platinum bikini worn by a stunningly gorgeous Eurasian model named Roxanne. It was yours for the bargain price of twelve thousand dollars. Mike looked at Carol and raised his eyebrows as if to say, "What do you think?" To my utter amazement, she nodded "Yes." He motioned to one of the attendants. There was a great deal of signaling and a lot of very fast-moving people and within minutes, Carol was presented with a beautifully wrapped twelve-thousand-dollar platinum bikini, which, I might add, she could wear to great advantage.

My week of R&R went by very fast, and late that last night, since I was heading back to Vietnam in the morning, Mike extracted a promise from me that I would visit him at his Galveston beach house on my way home from Vietnam. I promised that I would. To seal the deal, he gave me his AT&T credit card. I'm not making this up—I still have the card.

Chapter Thirty-Two

Houston Hall

One of my most unusual experiences as a Vietnam veteran occurred just after I was discharged from active duty in September of 1969. I had returned to the Hospital of the University of Pennsylvania to resume my surgical duties. The Penn campus, like so many other college campuses around the country, remained a hotbed of antiwar activity. I had already decided to concentrate on my surgery and to totally ignore the political scene. Imagine my surprise when I received a phone call from a medical student identifying himself as the president of the Student Medical Honor Society and inquiring as to medical care in Vietnam. I responded in the affirmative but added the caution that my experience was purely surgical and that I could only talk about that aspect of medical care. He said that was fine and to my surprise, after our conversation, I began seeing posters around campus advertising my appearance at the gathering.

I was originally scheduled to speak in a relatively small room, but the student called to tell me that because of the response they were getting, the event was being moved to Houston Hall, a larger room located in the heart of Penn's campus. I thanked him for the news and spent several days preparing my talk. I wanted to show a few slides depicting some minor wounds, avoiding any of the more serious injuries.

The evening before I was scheduled to appear, I received yet another call from the Honor Society president, who explained to me in a rather halting tone that if I wanted to back out of the talk, he would understand because he couldn't "guarantee my personal safety." After three months in Khe Sanh, the thought of confronting a few student hippies didn't faze me in the slightest. I told him in my strongest voice that I would be there and would be responsible for my own safety.

I would be lying if I said I didn't feel a bit on edge as

I walked into Houston Hall the evening of my talk. The room was packed mostly with students, many of them young men with long hair sporting all manner of headbands. I was introduced to virtually no applause and proceeded with my presentation. There was no sound as I spoke. At the end I invited questions. There were only a few and they were very much on the mild side, such as "Were you ever scared?" With reference to one of the casualty slides I had shown depicting leg wounds, someone asked, "Did that guy live?"

I assumed the evening was over, but a large group of students approached me as I was packing up my slides. I tensed a bit but relaxed when one of them, without a headband, asked if they could ask more questions. I sensed that they had been reluctant to do so in front of a larger audience. For the next hour or so I sat amongst them and discussed the details of my experiences caring for wounded Marines. They were extremely courteous and asked some really poignant questions. I remember one girl wanted to know if any of the men ever wrote to thank me for operating on them. I explained to her that I rarely, if ever, knew a casualty's name and that they only ever knew me as "Doc."

The evening ended with many quiet thank yous.. That is when I first created Finnegan's Rule #38—"Nothing dramatic ever happens."

Chapter Thirty-Three

I Was a Marine

I've always wanted to be able to say that but I can't. Even though I spent most of my two years on active duty with the Third Marine Division, most of that in Vietnam, and much of it under fire, I was nonetheless a Navy physician assigned to the Marines, but not a real Marine.

As I mentioned previously, I began my military life at Camp Lejuene, a U.S. Marine base in North Carolina, and went through six weeks of boot camp. This, however, was modified for us older and softer Navy doctors and was not nearly as difficult as what a real Marine boot went through. I couldn't call myself a Marine. I spent the last four months of 1967 at the Dong Ha combat base caring for Marine casualties and ducking fairly regular but relatively light incoming artillery fire. I was still just a Navy Doc in jungle fatigues.

From January through April 1968, even while I was the commanding officer of a surgical team stationed in Khe Sanh presiding over the care of over twenty-five hundred Marine casualties, and having been wounded myself (slightly), I still was not a Marine.

I have now written a book about my experiences with the Marines in Vietnam. As I was writing it, editing it, and rewriting it, I realized that the true story was not about me but rather about these highly trained, incredibly resourceful, absolutely fearless fighting machines they call the United States Marines.

Volunteers to a man, they manned the hills around us and fought the brutal "hill fights." With a "Quad-50," a half-track with a .50-caliber machine gun mounted on it, a squad of Marines sat on our perimeter just behind Charlie Med, as our triage bunkers were known at Khe Sanh. We had been told at boot camp that every grunt guarding our perimeter would die rather than let the NVA or Viet Cong get to the Navy doctors and corpsmen. I know this to be true. They are the Marines. I cared for so many of them with the most horrible of wounds: missing limbs, life-threatening injuries to the chest and abdomen, and other wounds to every imaginable part of the body. They seldom complained and if they spoke at all, it was almost always to ask about their buddies.

I've pretty much (realistically) abandoned my quest to be called a Marine. I know what their boot camp is like, and I don't know if I could have handled it. I've seen the wounds they sustained defending their positions and mine and I don't know if I have their kind of courage. I respect the tradition they have built with their blood, their honor, and their lives and I am content to have served with them, even if I can never truly be called a Marine.

Chapter Thirty-Four

Welcome Home

Anyone who lived in the good old U.S. of A. in the late 1960s, '70s, and '80s will attest to the widespread unpopularity of the war in Vietnam. Newspapers, magazine articles, novels, and movies highlighted this pervasive negativity and chronicled the scorn heaped on returning veterans. Instead of directing their anger at Congress and the White House, people across the country chose inexplicably to direct their anger and hostility toward the soldiers, sailors, and Marines who responded to their country's call. It was not easy to return from a year in a combat zone believing that you were there serving your country and trying to deter the spread of communism (Remember communism? It was very big back then) only to find that you were not only made to feel unwelcome but actually made to feel guilty about your service.

After my year in Vietnam, for which service I received several medals, including a Purple Heart and a Bronze Star with a Combat "V," I was assigned to the Philadelphia Naval Hospital. As part of our stateside briefing, we were advised to wear our uniforms only on the military base and to wear civilian clothes when off the base.

In June of 1968, it was necessary for me to leave the Naval Hospital to drive a few miles into West Philadelphia, the location of the Hospital of the University of Pennsylvania to which I would return upon my discharge from the Navy in September of 1969. The paperwork I had to complete would take less than an hour, after which I would return to the Naval Hospital to finish my day's work. I decided to stay in uniform, which was summer dress khakis with shoulder boards and ribbons. I parked my car, entered the lobby of the Ravdin Building, and got onto an elevator to go up to the offices of the Department of Surgery. One of my professors, a man in his mid-fifties who had never been in the service, nodded his recognition and then, in front of several other occupants of the elevator, reached over, touched my ribbons, and said, with a southern drawl, "Jim, did you earn those or buy them?" Just as he made the comment, the elevator door opened and he walked off. No one else said a word. I don't recall my thoughts at that precise moment but it must have been about that time that I decided, consciously or subconsciously, to keep my Vietnam experience to myself.

Fast-forward about thirty years. All of my children are grown and married and I am now divorced and remarried, this time to my darling Linda who is my soulmate, my inspiration, and the driving force behind this book. At Christmastime, my daughter Maureen and her husband Mark invited Linda and I to have dinner with them and Mark's parents. We were seated at a circular table at the Krazy Kat restaurant in Wilmington, Delaware. I was next to Mark's dad, who is about my age. He is a man who is very easy to talk to, and at that moment, I found myself discussing the library at LaSalle University in Philadelphia, which housed a special collection on Vietnam dedicated to the art and literature produced around the time of the war. I had actually been invited to LaSalle on a few occasions to sit in on a senior honors seminar dedicated to my war.

I was delighted to learn that many of these college seniors seemed to have a sincere interest in learning about this conflict. Many of them had fathers and uncles who had been there. Mark's dad, Paul, then began asking about my one-year tour and I responded without hesitation. After a while, it became apparent that everyone at the table had stopped talking and was listening to my discussion with Paul. I started to apologize for monopolizing the conversation when my daughter, Maureen, interrupted me and said, "Dad, please don't stop. This is the first time in thirty years that I've ever even heard you speak of Vietnam."

Chapter Thirty-Five

A Final Thought

Lt. Col. William Gay, US Army (Ret)

L t. Bill Gay was one of many Marines wounded in Khe Sanh. He is a true hero and I tell some of his story elsewhere in this book. Bill was interviewed last year by Jan Herman, who served for thirty years as the editor of *Navy Medicine.* Jan has published several books, his most recent titled *Navy Medicine in Vietnam,* an excellent read that includes the interview with Bill Gay, who is now Lt. Col. William Gay, U.S. Army (ret). Jan and Bill have graciously allowed me to reproduce part of that interview here.

It was only when we arrived in Phu Bai or Dong Ha, I can't remember which, that I heard what happened. When we were taking off from Khe Sanh, mortar rounds began coming in. As the kids who were carrying the last stretcher for the last medevac pushed that stretcher onto the chopper and turned to leave, a mortar round went off and wounded both of them. The crew chief jumped out, picked up these two men, and threw them into this last bird as it took off. That was a typical day in Khe Sanh.

At Khe Sanh, Charlie Med was a complete subculture with amazing people. When the siege started, those doctors were operating behind sand bag walls that weren't even full height.

Prior to the Seabees building a bunker for them, the doctors were operating in different places so they all wouldn't be killed at one time. The number of people they treated and then medevaced out was just unbelievable. It was a constant conveyor belt of injured and mangled people. Those medical folks just worked day and night.

On most days I had one of my men posted down at Charlie Med with a "shopping list." He had a list of boot sizes we needed, a list of pants, shirts, and flak jackets. As the wounded came in and their clothing was thrown in a heap, one of my men would pick it up because we needed replacement clothing.

Charlie Med took care of our men. I had one corpsman who was assigned to my platoon. And when he wasn't helping us, he was running over to someone nearby who was wounded and patching him up enough so we could get him to Charlie Med.

I can't tell you how important Charlie Med was to the morale of all of us at Khe Sanh. We as combat engineers—that always had to expose us to move about the combat base—found some extra courage to do so because we believed that if we were wounded, we would survive if our platoon mates could only get us to Charlie Med.

If I were to title this history, I'd call it, "Just Get Me to Charlie Med . . . . . . They'll Save Me." You need to believe in something positive to find the courage to keep fighting every day in the face of incoming rockets, artillery, mortars, recoilless rifle fire, and well-aimed rifle fire from disciplined and well-trained North Vietnamese Regular Army forces.

The young Navy corpsmen that lived with us and the

doctors at Charlie Med gave us that positive belief. David Douglas Duncan's "I Protest," his photo history of the carnage at Khe Sanh, includes a photo of the doctors of Charlie Med doing major surgery while dressed in full combat gear in a dirty, dimly lit bunker. I personally saw events like that occur. I marveled at the focus, skill, and dedication of those doctors then. Quite frankly, I can't remember those scenes today without my eyes filling with tears of gratitude.

I can say this, many more people would have died at Khe Sanh had it not been for the doctors in Charlie Med and the corpsmen and Marines who volunteered to put us on the choppers. It was the story of the young Marine with the mortar round in his stomach being saved that was heard throughout Khe Sanh that led to the mantra, "Get me to Charlie Med . . . They'll save me."

Chapter Thirty-Six

Kevin

The following essay was written by my grandson, Kevin Finnegan, in his senior year in high school. His assignment was to write about some person or event that influenced his life. Reading it brought tears to my eyes.

A Bloodline of Service

Pittsburgh has forever been a city associated with hard work. It was, and still is, a tough blue-collar city, and it is also the home to my grandfather, Dr. James O. Finnegan, M.D., or Pop-Pop, as we all call him. Born and raised in the "steel city," he was educated at Pittsburgh Central Catholic High School for Boys and later graduated from La Salle College and Hahnemann Medical School, both in Philadelphia. Regardless of his schooling, it is my grandfather's personality and his dedication to the service of others that has influenced me so greatly in my life. It is his story that I admire dearly and would like to live up to in my lifetime.

The year is 1967 and the Vietnam War is reaching its peak. After medical school, my grandfather did something that very few people at the time were willing to do: he volunteered to join the service (the U.S. Naval Reserve). I remember my sophomore year in high school when he came into my history class to discuss his experience in Vietnam with us and he said one thing that I will never forget. As a young boy, his father told him that if there ever was one thing you should do in your lifetime, it should be to serve your country. He did live up to this statement. Following rigorous training by the Marine Corps to become a naval combat surgeon, he was shipped out to South Vietnam, where he was stationed with the Third Marine Division. The place where he was stationed, Marine Fire Base Khe Sanh, was besieged by nearly 30,000 North Vietnamese soldiers. This is where his service to others comes to light.

As a surgeon, his job was to treat wounded Marines in the operating room, and care for them in the triage. He would often operate in bunkers of sandbags, with constant enemy artillery bombarding the base. He would even risk his own life to unload Marine casualties out of landing helicopters while under heavy enemy fire. He was even wounded by artillery shrapnel because of his actions. My grandfather returned from Vietnam in the fall of 1968, and was awarded the Purple Heart for wounds received in combat and the Bronze Star for courageous actions during combat. He then returned home to his family to continue his medical career in the civilian sector, where he became a renowned heart and lung surgeon in the area.

I too feel this strong desire to serve, not only to serve others, but also my country. My grandfather's service to his country, and all those who have served this country, is something that I will forever admire. Ever since I was in grade school, I have felt this calling, a calling to help others, to serve others. I want to do things with my life that will ensure the aid of those in need. I want to help those who struggle and grant them happiness and success, and there is no other way I want to do this than to serve my country. I would like to achieve this through the means of an ROTC scholarship, or even Officer Candidate School, or the Reserves, for either the Army or Marine Corps. Regardless of the path chosen, I will say this, and I do not hesitate to say it: I am willing to put all that I am, and my own life at risk to help others. I am willing to put the welfare of others before my own and that is why the armed forces are called the service, and that is why I want to join. Even after the service, I would greatly like to carry this lifestyle of service into a job in the field of law enforcement, through a criminal justice degree.

I am and always will be this type of person: kind, caring, compassionate, selfless, and hardworking. I always try to pick up my friends when they are down, and I never judge others for their differences. I work to the best of my ability both academically, devoting much time to school work and studying, and athletically, spending hours on end lifting weights and running sprints for the upcoming football season. I was even selected by one of my football coaches to be a member of a leadership class, to instill in us the values found in a leader.

This dedication, hard work, and selfless care for others, I did not learn alone. It has been my grandfather's influence that has pushed me to develop my strong character and high level of integrity. He is a model, a template for which I want to live my own life, and I will forever cherish the principles for which he has lived his life.

Kevin Finnegan

2006

Ed Feldmann and the author - 1968

Ed Feldman and the author - 2008

EPILOGUE

The siege of Khe Sanh took place forty-one years ago. The war in Vietnam ended thirty-four years ago. Since then, hundreds of books and magazine articles have been published about that "conflict." Several television documentaries highlighted various aspects of the war. Public television aired a particularly good program detailing the Khe Sanh siege. It ended with footage showing the complete dismantling and leveling of that once-famous outpost. I remember feeling dumbstruck and incredibly sad as I watched it. In the end, it seemed as though we were never there—no airstrip, no bunkers, no Marines, no Charlie Med. Nothing to remind us of the twenty-five hundred casualties we had treated. Not one cross or helmet to remember the dead Marines who fought so gallantly to defend the base and us. I can't help asking why. Did we win anything? Did we save anything or anybody? Did we alter the fate of the Vietnamese people? Is the world a better place because brave, young American Marines fought and died on this tiny plateau and the surrounding hills? Have the disabilities resulting from thousands of wounds been properly treated and hopefully lessened? Answers? Anyone?

Here's what I know. Nineteen-year-old corporals do not declare war. Young lieutenants and captains who lead platoons and companies into battle do not choose those battles. They just fight them. Presidents and senators and congressmen declare or authorize war. They seldom if ever fight them. They love making speeches about them. Many of them have never served in the military. The majority have never seen combat.

Here's what I wish. I wish there would never be another war.

Vietnam Soldiers

Risked your life
Made a sacrifice
Gave it all you got
Wounds or hatred didn't stop you
You kept going

And for that.......
We thank You

— Caitlin 2000
Finnegan age: 11